A DOCTOR'S LIFE

A Visual History of Doctors and Nurses
through the Ages

Rod Storring

Heinemann

First published in Great Britain in 1998
by Heinemann Library,
a division of Reed Educational and Professional
Publishing Limited,
Halley Court, Jordan Hill, Oxford, OX2 8EJ.

Heinemann is a registered trademark of Reed Educational
and Professional Publishing Limited

MADRID ATHENS FLORENCE PRAGUE
WARSAW PORTSMOUTH NH CHICAGO
SAO PAULO MEXICO SINGAPORE TOKYO
MELBOURNE AUCKLAND IBADAN
GABORONE JOHANNESBURG KAMPALA
NAIROBI

ISBN 0 431 02300 X (Hardback)
ISBN 0 431 02248 4 (Paperback)

A CIP catalogue record for this book is available at the
British Library.

Printed in Spain

Conceived and produced by Breslich & Foss Ltd, London
Series Editor: Laura Wilson
Editor: Janet Ravenscroft
Art Director: Nigel Osborne
Design: Paul Cooper Design
Photography: Miki Slingsby

CONTENTS

ROMAN DOCTOR c.50 AD

Lucius Spectatus

Lucius Spectatus was an army doctor attached to Legion XIV which was serving in Britain. His rank was that of *Centurio Valetudinarian* (Centurion of the Hospital). A Roman by birth, Lucius was apprenticed to a doctor who looked after wounded gladiators, so he was expert at dealing with wounds from swords and spears and stopping bleeding – very useful skills for an army doctor. He joined the army when he was 27, after finishing his medical apprenticeship. He was dismayed to be sent to Britain, but after a while he grew used to the wet weather.

Like all Roman doctors, Lucius's training was based on Greek medicine, particularly the teachings of Hippocrates (*c*.400 BC) whose followers wrote over 60 medical books, which are called the 'Hippocratic Corpus'. Lucius was familiar with the instructions they gave for curing illness and knew that to treat a patient properly, he must do four things. These were: diagnosing (asking about the patient's symptoms in order to work out what is wrong); making a prognosis (considering what is likely to happen if the symptoms continue); observing (checking the patient to see how he was getting on and modifying treatment if necessary); and, finally, treating the patient. Modern doctors still follow this practice *(see page 41)*. As dissecting (cutting open and examining) bodies was forbidden at this time, Lucius knew little about anatomy (the physical structure of the body), which limited his medical knowledge.

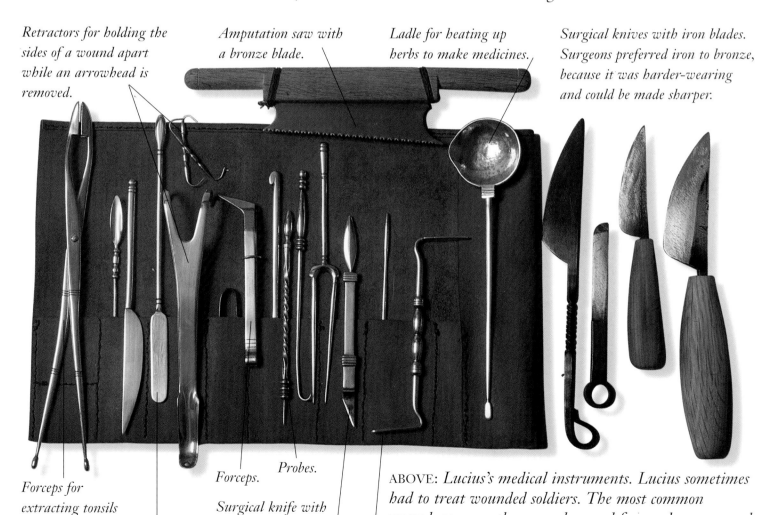

Retractors for holding the sides of a wound apart while an arrowhead is removed.

Amputation saw with a bronze blade.

Ladle for heating up herbs to make medicines.

Surgical knives with iron blades. Surgeons preferred iron to bronze, because it was harder-wearing and could be made sharper.

Forceps for extracting tonsils and haemorrhoids.

Probe for exploring wounds.

Forceps.

Probes.

Surgical knife with an iron blade and a bronze handle.

Tool for lifting organs out of the way during surgery.

ABOVE: *Lucius's medical instruments. Lucius sometimes had to treat wounded soldiers. The most common wounds were on the arms, legs and face and were caused by arrowheads, which usually had to be removed. Lucius could also set broken bones and repair dislocated ones. He performed some other operations, such as removing tumours and haemorrhoids.*

THE FOUR HUMOURS

The Greeks believed that the body contained four fluids, or 'humours': blood, phlegm, yellow bile and black bile. If a person had too much or too little of any one of these humours, they would become ill – to have good health, they needed to be kept in balance. The humours were associated with particular elements and qualities (symptoms):

HUMOUR	ELEMENT	QUALITIES
Blood	Air	Hot and wet
Phlegm	Water	Cold and wet
Yellow bile	Fire	Hot and dry
Black bile	Earth	Cold and dry

Medicine based on the four humours was still being practised in Europe as late as the 17th century.

RIGHT: *Lucius's wax tablet for making notes, often written by the light of an oil lamp.*

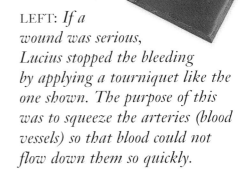

LEFT: *If a wound was serious, Lucius stopped the bleeding by applying a tourniquet like the one shown. The purpose of this was to squeeze the arteries (blood vessels) so that blood could not flow down them so quickly.*

GALEN

The great medical authority of this time was a Roman doctor called Galen. Born in AD 129, he studied at the medical school in Alexandria and later became physician (doctor) to the Roman Emperor. He dissected pigs and monkeys to learn about anatomy. Animals' bodies are not the same as human bodies, but thanks to his experiments Galen added a great deal to existing anatomical knowledge. In Europe, his work was considered the basis of medicine for over 1,000 years and few doctors dared to contradict his teachings.

KNIGHT HOSPITALLER c.1200

Richard, Member of the Order of the Hospital of St John of Jerusalem

Richard, who came from a rich family, joined a crusade to the Holy Land when he was 18. He wanted to help defend Jerusalem, the site of Christ's crucifixion, from the Muslims. While he was there he joined the Knights Hospitallers. The Hospitallers were one of two orders of military monks who made up the permanent Christian fighting force in the Holy Land. Their purpose was not only to fight the Muslims, but also to care for sick and wounded pilgrims and crusaders. Richard, who took vows of poverty, chastity and obedience, felt that by fighting the Muslims and caring for the sick, he was serving God well.

The Hospitallers were based at St John's hospital in Jerusalem. Their aim, like that of the few other hospitals that existed at the time, was to provide a comfortable place for sick people, with good nursing care, in the hope that they would get well by themselves. The Hospitallers did not take an active part in the cure by giving drugs or performing surgery.

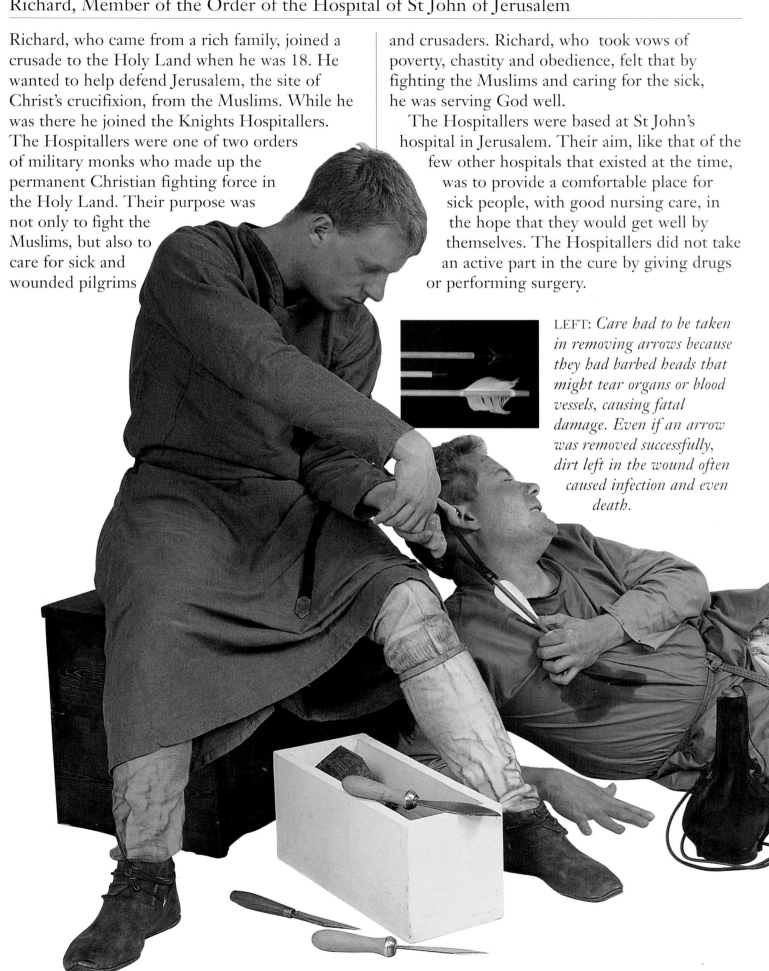

LEFT: *Care had to be taken in removing arrows because they had barbed heads that might tear organs or blood vessels, causing fatal damage. Even if an arrow was removed successfully, dirt left in the wound often caused infection and even death.*

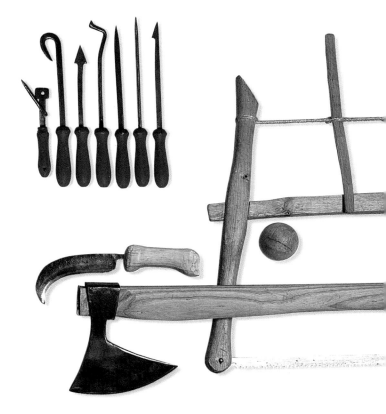

ABOVE: *Flasks and herb jars with a pestle and mortar. Islamic medicine made great use of plant substances, including laudanum (opium) and senna, which is still used as a laxative today.*

RIGHT: *A selection of surgical tools. The hammer and chisel in the small picture (centre) were used to amputate fingers. The saw and axe were used to amputate arms and legs.*

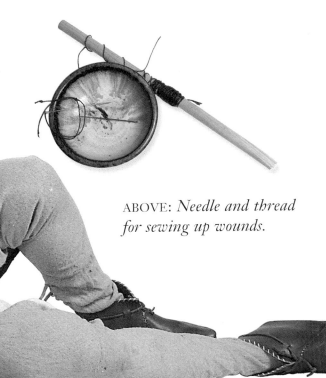

ABOVE: *Needle and thread for sewing up wounds.*

LEFT: *Richard had not had any medical training before he joined the Hospitallers, and he had to learn 'on the job'. Knights were frequently wounded by arrows and crossbow bolts, and these had to be pulled out with pliers.*

ISLAMIC MEDICINE

The Crusaders soon realised that the Islamic doctors were better than their own. The Hospitallers, a rich order, used some of their money to employ skilled Islamic doctors to care for the wounded.

Like European medicine, Islamic medicine was based on the teachings of Hippocrates and Galen (*see pages 4 and 5*), which had been translated into the Arabic language. Islamic medicine was better regulated than it was in Western Europe, with hospitals, medical schools and a requirement that doctors should pass an examination before they could practise medicine. The two most famous Arab doctors were Rhazes (860-932), who wrote a medical encyclopedia, and Avicenna (979–1037), whose book *The Canon of Medicine* was translated into Latin, and used by both Islamic and Western doctors for over 500 years.

ABOVE and BELOW: *To prepare herbal medicines, Richard measured out quantities of herbs which he distilled in an alembic (see page 15).*

MONASTIC MEDICINE c.1200

Brother Dominic and Sister Clare

Brother Dominic, a Benedictine monk, was trained in medicine by a monk physician who taught him the theories of Hippocrates and Galen *(see pages 4 and 5)*. He also learnt how to do blood letting and cupping, how to give purgatives and diuretics *(see Glossary)*, and how illnesses could be treated with herbs. He worked in the monastery's infirmary, treating sick monks, and also in a hospital outside the monastery gates, where he treated members of the public. Sister Clare, a nun in the order of the Poor Clares, also worked in a hospital, treating female patients. Like all medieval people, Brother Dominic and Sister Clare believed that sickness was God's way of punishing sinful people, but they considered that caring for the sick was an act of Christian charity and that prayer was the best cure. Saints were associated with particular illnesses; for example, if Brother Dominic had a patient with a sore eye, he prayed to St Lucy, and if his patient had a throat complaint, he offered his prayers to St Blaise.

ABOVE: *Brother Dominic treated his patients with herbs grown in the monastery's herb garden. These were dried and ground up by mortar and pestle and then stored in clay pots or wooden chests until needed.*

LEFT: *Medicinal herbs (from the top):* box, tansy, mugwort, cotton lavender, yarrow, fennel, meadowsweet, rosemary, hedge-woundwort *and* southernwood.

Brother Dominic and Sister Clare prepare remedies. Several 'nursing orders' of nuns were founded in medieval times. Until the 20th century, most of the nurses in Europe were nuns.

BLOOD LETTING

According to Hippocrates' teachings, a patient with a fever might have too much blood in his body. This would destroy the balance of his humours (*see page 5*) and make him hot and sometimes excitable or angry. During medieval and Tudor times it was believed that removing or 'letting' some of the blood would not only lower the patient's temperature, but also make him calmer. It was also believed that poisons could be removed in this way. The patient's skin was pierced, cut or cupped and the blood allowed to flow out. Blood letting was still practised in the 19th century, with some doctors advising that patients should be bled until they fainted. This is not a good idea, as a sick person can be fatally weakened by the loss of so much blood.

Another method of blood letting, also still practised widely in the 19th century, was to apply leeches to the patient's skin and allow them to bite him and drink his blood.

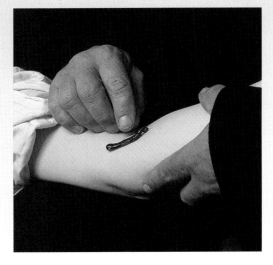

ABOVE: *A leech can drink three times its own weight in blood and survive for up to a year afterwards without another meal. Its saliva contains a substance called hirudin which prevents blood from clotting.*

BARBER-SURGEON c.1450

John Mason

A distinction has been made between medicine and surgery ever since the time of Hippocrates. The Greek word for surgery, *chirurgia*, means 'work of the hand' and for many years it was considered to be inferior to medicine, which was more intellectual. Although surgeons were not thought as important as physicians (doctors), by the 15th century they had their own guild, the Company of Barber-Surgeons. Members of the guild earned money from cutting hair, shaving and dentistry as well as from performing operations.

John Mason learnt his trade by spending five years apprenticed to a master of the Company of Barber-Surgeons. He passed the examination to become a guild member, and set up his own practice in York.

Most people could not afford to pay a physician and relied on apothecaries (*see page 15*) and barber-surgeons to treat them. John Mason considered himself to be a craftsman like his neighbour Gilbert, the carpenter, and was proud that his skills were recognised by local physicians, who asked him to bleed their patients.

ABOVE: *Shaving kit: soap made from sage and olive oil, a sponge, a razor and a bowl.*

LEFT: *Fresh herbs for making medicines.*

BELOW: *The most common way of discovering what was wrong with a patient was to examine his urine. The chart below shows that the smell, colour and even taste of the urine were all considered important to the diagnosis of a person's illness.*

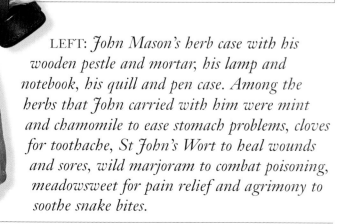

LEFT: *John Mason's herb case with his wooden pestle and mortar, his lamp and notebook, his quill and pen case. Among the herbs that John carried with him were mint and chamomile to ease stomach problems, cloves for toothache, St John's Wort to heal wounds and sores, wild marjoram to combat poisoning, meadowsweet for pain relief and agrimony to soothe snake bites.*

LEFT: *John Mason's medical kit included bandages, needles and thread, tooth extractors and prickers for removing splinters.*

BELOW: *John Mason was an expert tooth extractor and bone setter, and he used these skills frequently. This was because many people had rotten teeth and there were frequent accidents such as falls from horses and brawls in the local taverns. He also performed operations on bladder stones, certain types of hernias and cataracts in the eyes.*

TUDOR NAVAL SURGEON c.1540

William Iron

Having been apprenticed to a barber-surgeon, William Iron joined His Majesty's Navy during the reign of King Henry VIII. He wanted to learn more about surgery and to save some money in order to settle down in England and set up in practice as a barber-surgeon.

As a naval surgeon, William Iron had to look after the general health of the sailors and treat those who were wounded in battle. The battlefield was known as 'the school for surgery'. It was where surgeons learnt to deal with many types of wounds and where most advances were made in surgical techniques. One of the most important developments was made by a French doctor called Ambroise Paré.

Until the mid-16th century, gunshot wounds were either burnt with a hot iron called a cautery or filled with boiling oil. These treatments were thought to prevent the shot poisoning the patient. However, Paré discovered that patients whose wounds were not treated like this recovered better, and eventually the practice was stopped.

THEORY AND PRACTICE

William Iron's understanding of medicine was based on Hippocrates' teachings (*see page 4*) and he did not think much of modern physicians, especially those teaching at universities. This was, he said, because they only talked about medicine, and never put their theories into practice by treating people.

BELOW: *William Iron treated his patients with herbal salves and poultices that he made himself.*

Fleams for bleeding patients.

Hammer, used with chisel for amputating fingers.

Saw for cutting through bones.

Tool for hooking out blood vessels after an amputation (see opposite).

Salve to help wounds heal.

Forceps for removing gunshot.

Curved knife for cutting through skin and muscle.

OPPOSITE: *In the days before anaesthetics (substances that cause loss of feeling), surgery was horrifically painful. An amputation had to be carried out right after the injury, while the patient was still in a state of shock. Otherwise the double shock of the injury and the operation would be too much and the patient would die.*

If a sailor's arm or leg was hit by gunshot, William Iron would probably have to amputate it (cut it off). If left, the limb could become infected and the sailor would die from blood-poisoning or gangrene. William was proud of the speed of his amputations. For an arm amputation, he would not take more than four minutes. First, he cut through the flesh on the arm with a curved knife, then he sawed through the bone with a saw. Then he used a crook-shaped tool to pull out the ends of the blood vessels from the wound and tied up the ends to stop the patient bleeding to death.

ELIZABETHAN HOUSEWIFE c.1590

Mistress Bailey

Alice Bailey was the wife of a rich merchant. As well as looking after her house and garden and overseeing her servants, she gave medicines to her family and to poor people in the local villages who could not afford to go to the apothecary *(see opposite)*. Like many wealthy Elizabethan women, Mistress Bailey regarded this as an important part of her religious duty. She had a reputation for curing illness, and many people asked her advice.

Mistress Bailey agreed with the apothecaries and physicians that the way to be healthy was to keep the four humours in balance *(see page 5)*.

If there were any blockages in the body – if, for example, a person was constipated – this might cause a build-up of one particular humour, alter the balance and make the person ill.

To remove the blockage and cure the patient, Mistress Bailey often gave people emetics (to make them vomit) and laxative medicines. Vomiting was thought to be good because it got rid of bad things in the stomach before they could make the whole body sick.

ABOVE and LEFT: *Medicinal herbs.*

BELOW: *Comfits made by Mistress Bailey: rosecakes made of pounded rose petals, sugar and gum tragacanth were used to treat headaches; lozenges called troches were for sore throats.*

THE DOCTRINE OF SIGNATURES

Like many people, Alice Bailey believed that there must be a medicinal substance to treat every disease, and that something about that substance – usually its appearance – would indicate which illness it should be used for.

For example, red wine was thought to be a good treatment for someone who had lost a lot of blood. This theory was called the doctrine of signatures, or signs.

ABOVE: *Alice Bailey made lavender water by distillation, using an alembic. Distillation is the process of evaporating liquid (making it into a vapour) and then condensing it. This means that the distilled herb water is very strong. First, Alice put bunches of lavender in boiling water in the bottom half of the alembic (above left). The dish under the alembic contained hot coals to keep the water boiling. Next Alice put the lid on to contain the steam which rose from the boiling water (above centre).*

Finally, she wrapped the top of the alembic in wet cloths to cool it (above right). When the cloths dried out she poured more cold water on them. This cooling action condensed the steam inside the alembic lid. The steam turned into droplets of liquid which fell down, collected on the narrow rim inside the lid, then dripped out of the spout.

APOTHECARIES

Apothecaries were people who made up medicines and sold them to the public. People went to an apothecary's shop, told him about their illness and asked him which medicine they should take. Apothecaries did not charge for giving advice, so the majority of people, who were not rich enough to hire physicians, went to them for help. Like Mistress Bailey's medicines, the apothecaries' potions consisted mainly of herbs and spices, although some contained powdered bones, blood and tree bark.

LEFT: *Mistress Bailey mixed her own medicine. She kept the spices in a locked chest, to which only she had the key. She did all the work herself because she did not trust her servants with such expensive goods. One nutmeg, for example, cost six pence, which was a day's wage for a labourer.*

PLAGUE DOCTOR 1665

John Watson

John Watson was one of the few doctors who did not leave London when plague broke out in 1665. Rich Londoners went away, taking their doctors with them, but John had just set up his practice, so did not have any rich patients. Soon John was exhausted from treating so many plague victims.

He knew that there was a high risk of getting the plague if he stayed in London, but he thought his uniform, which covered every part of his body, would protect him. Like all physicians, John thought that the plague was passed on by contact with 'miasma' or bad air. The beak on his mask is stuffed with spices and dried flowers to sweeten it.

In fact, plague was carried by rat fleas that were infected with plague bacillus (bacteria which cause disease). There were many rats in London, and their fleas bit people and gave them the plague. The plague has three human types. In bubonic plague, the patient gets swellings called buboes. These swellings start under the armpits and around the groin and spread to other parts of the body. The bacilli can also enter the bloodstream, causing blood poisoning, or they can affect the lungs, causing pneumonic plague, which can be spread by sneezing and coughing. In the last stages of all types of the plague, black bruises appear on the skin, which was why it was originally called the Black Death.

QUARANTINE

Like the Black Death, which spread through Europe in 1347-49, the Great Plague of London killed thousands of people. About 20 per cent of the population died of it. Although most people believed, like John Watson, that the plague was spread by bad air, they also thought that they might catch it from going near people who already had it.

When a case of plague was discovered, the victim and his or her family were locked in their house for 40 days so that they could not pass on the infection. Their door was marked with a red cross so that people would avoid it. This method of isolating people is called keeping them in quarantine.

ABOVE: *John Watson told his patients to keep plenty of flowers and spices in their houses to improve the bad air, and he used powdered bones, toads, snakes and tree bark as medicines. He tried his best to cure his patients, but most of them died. Before he left his patients, he told them to pray to God to have mercy on their souls and allow them to live.*

MᶜLEAN'S MONTHLY SHEF

...ES ·THE VICTOR ᵺ THE VANQUISH'D BOTH.

ABOVE: *Epidemics (widespread diseases) like the plague continued to strike Europe from time to time. This illustration from 1817 warns people about cholera, which was caused by drinking infected water. Cholera was highly contagious and killed thousands of people during the 19th century, especially in crowded cities (see page 22). Ships arriving in the United States with European immigrants were turned away if it was suspected that there might be cholera on board.*

BELOW: *Scenes showing people burying the dead during the 1665 plague.*

John Dunstall fecit.

RESURRECTIONIST *c.1750*

Jeremiah Clinker

During the day Jeremiah Clinker worked as a messenger, but at night he crept into churchyards and dug up bodies. He sold them to a teacher at the medical school who wanted them so that his students could have real bodies to dissect. Jeremiah was known as a resurrection man because he brought bodies back from the dead, or a 'body snatcher' or 'grave robber'.

The law on dissection (*see opposite*) meant that there were few dead bodies available for the medical students to practise on, and resurrection men realised they could make a lot of money by supplying them. What Jeremiah was doing was illegal, and if caught he would have been fined.

At this time, bodies were buried, not cremated (burnt), and people thought that they would not get into heaven if their body had been cut into pieces. Nowadays, many people do not believe this and leave their bodies to science or carry donor cards so that, when they die, their organs can be transplanted into someone else's body to help that person to live longer.

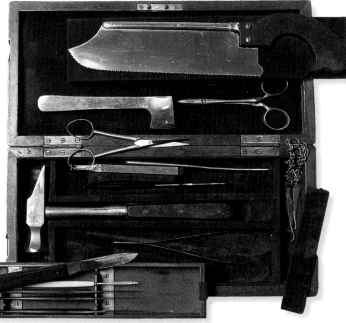

ABOVE and RIGHT: *Eighteenth and 19th century post-mortem kits for cutting up bodies. 'Post mortem' is a Latin term meaning 'after death'. Bodies were sometimes cut up to find out the cause of death if it was not obvious to the doctor.*

BELOW: *Body snatchers needed to provide fresh corpses, so they spied on churchyards to see when funerals were being held and returned after dark to collect the bodies. There were some grave robbers, however, who murdered people in order to sell their bodies to the medical schools. The best known of these are Burke and Hare, who supplied the famous Scottish anatomist Robert Knox with corpses until they were caught in 1828.*

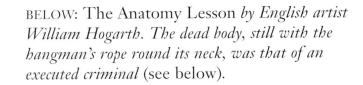

BELOW: The Anatomy Lesson *by English artist William Hogarth. The dead body, still with the hangman's rope round its neck, was that of an executed criminal* (see below).

THE STUDY OF ANATOMY

For many years, the human body was considered to be sacred, and dissecting it was forbidden. This made it difficult for doctors to learn about both anatomy (the structure and contents of the body) and physiology (how the body works). In 1543, an Italian, Andreas Vesalius, published a book called *The Fabric of the Human Body*, with drawings of bodies that he had dissected. When doctors saw it, they realised that the anatomy in Galen's books *(see page 5)* was wrong, and that they needed to cut open real human bodies and study the contents in order to make medical progress. However, it was very hard to get hold of a body, and most people thought that dissection was wicked.

In Britain in Henry VII's time, the bodies of executed criminals were given to medical schools for dissection, because it was considered to be a further punishment after death. Anatomy laws passed in the 19th century in Europe and the USA gave medical schools permission to use unclaimed bodies (usually of very poor people) for dissection. Many thought that this was unfair, because it was 'punishing' people for being poor.

MEDICINE MAN c.1860

Four Elks

Four Elks was a Plains Indian from the Cheyenne tribe who lived on the central plains of North America. Plains Indians believed that everything in the world was part of one Great Spirit and was a potential source of the spiritual power they called 'medicine'. The medicine man held a very important position in his village, because he had the power both to heal people physically and to restore their spirit. To do this, he used a mixture of rituals, such as dances and pipe-smoking ceremonies, and herbs which were either medicinal or considered to have magic powers. Besides herbs, the sun, moon and sky were thought to have magic powers. American Indian 'medicine' was used for prevention as well as cure. A warrior carried 'medicine bundles' of sacred objects or painted special symbols on his shield, which he believed would protect him from injury while out hunting buffalo or fighting in battle.

Each member of the tribe had his or her own particular sacred objects, such as a special stone or piece of wood (*see left*), that they had found, or a symbol that had appeared to them in a dream. These objects would protect and cure them.

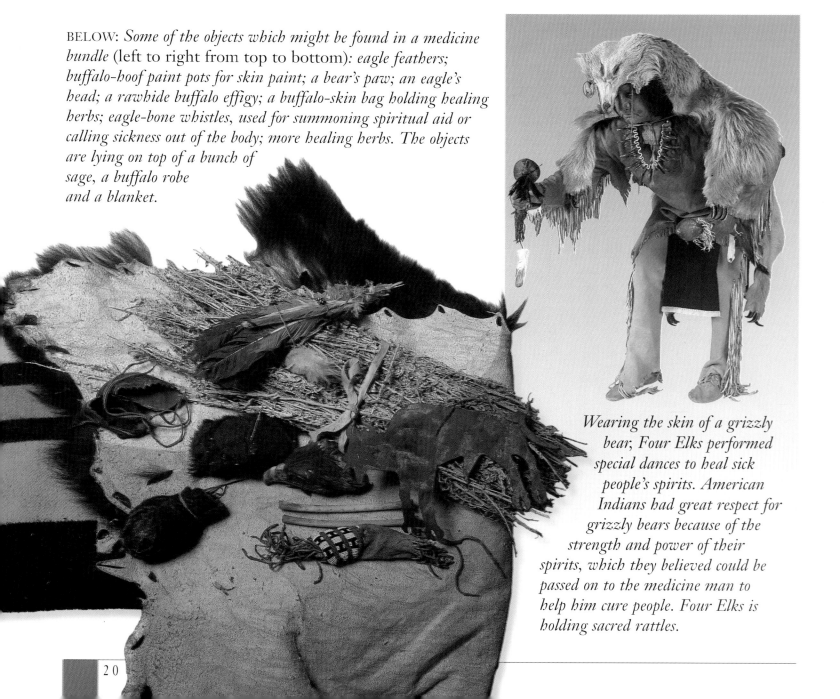

BELOW: *Some of the objects which might be found in a medicine bundle* (left to right from top to bottom): *eagle feathers; buffalo-hoof paint pots for skin paint; a bear's paw; an eagle's head; a rawhide buffalo effigy; a buffalo-skin bag holding healing herbs; eagle-bone whistles, used for summoning spiritual aid or calling sickness out of the body; more healing herbs. The objects are lying on top of a bunch of sage, a buffalo robe and a blanket.*

Wearing the skin of a grizzly bear, Four Elks performed special dances to heal sick people's spirits. American Indians had great respect for grizzly bears because of the strength and power of their spirits, which they believed could be passed on to the medicine man to help him cure people. Four Elks is holding sacred rattles.

Long 'medicine' ceremonies took place in sweat lodges like this one. Water was poured over hot stones to create steam. The men took off their clothes and sat in a circle to purify themselves by sweating. Warriors often took part in ceremonies to help their injuries to heal.

NEW DISEASES

Before the arrival of Europeans, the native people of North America had never come into contact with diseases such as measles, cholera and influenza, so they had no natural immunity to them (ability to resist disease). When Christopher Columbus's expedition arrived on the American continent in 1492, it brought many of these diseases with it. When the Spaniards came into contact with the American Indians, they passed diseases on, causing many millions of deaths.

Eventually, those who survived these diseases developed an immunity to them, which they passed on to their children. Having an immunity meant that, if they did catch the disease, they would not be so seriously ill and would probably survive it.

RIGHT: *Four Elks burns sage on a piece of buffalo dung and fans the smoke towards him with an eagle wing fan. It was thought that drawing smoke towards you increased both physical and spiritual strength.*
Many Plains Indian ceremonies made use of tobacco, which was regarded as a sacred herb and smoked in pipes. Four Elks is sitting on a buffalo robe, and there is a grizzly bear skin hanging over his backrest.

VICTORIAN PUBLIC HEALTH

During the Industrial Revolution, in the late 18th and early 19th centuries, many country-dwellers moved into towns to work in the new factories. The parts of towns where these workers lived soon became overcrowded and dirty. Their homes had no proper toilets or bathrooms and very little clean running water. The filthy streets attracted large numbers of fleas, bed bugs and rats. In general, people did not have enough nourishing food to eat and were not in good health. As a result, they had little resistance to the germs that spread diseases. Many poor people died of typhoid, cholera, tuberculosis and influenza. It was not until scientists and doctors began to understand more about the way germs carry illnesses, and the importance of clean water, that conditions began to improve *(see page 28)*. However, the lack of a remedy against such infectious diseases continued to be a problem into the 20th century.

In America, a cook called Mary Mallon carried the disease of typhoid without showing any symptoms of it herself for over 15 years. In that time she started a series of epidemics in which over 2,000 people died. When she was identified and caught, she was sentenced to spend the rest of her life in quarantine in a hospital. She was known in the newspapers as 'Typhoid Mary'.

ABOVE and RIGHT: *Sewage and factory waste in the rivers was not the only pollution problem in the 19th century. In towns, air quality was poor because coal fires in people's homes and factory chimneys gave off smoke and fumes. Sometimes this 'smog' made it hard to see.*

LEFT: *Poor people's houses did not have inside toilets. Even in wealthy people's homes, chamber pots like this one were kept under the bed for use at night and emptied by the servants in the morning.*

MIDWIFE c.1860

Martha Sharpe

Although Martha Sharpe was not trained in midwifery, she had had nine children of her own so she knew a lot about childbirth. At first, it was just neighbours who asked her to come to their houses and help when their children were born, but after a few years she was able to make a living from it. Martha knew that the doctors – all male – who delivered babies disapproved of her old-fashioned methods. Martha thought that doctors killed more women and babies with their fancy instruments, such as forceps *(below)*, than they saved. Martha had no instruments or pain-relief. If the woman giving birth screamed in pain, Martha gave her a rolled-up towel and told her to bite hard on it.

Childbirth in the days before anaesthesia and asepsis (see pages 26 and 29) *was very dangerous. It was not unknown for women to die from blood loss or from an infection they had caught during the birth. There were some useful instruments, such as this vectis* (right), *which was used to help push the baby into the correct position if it was lying the wrong way for a normal birth.*

However, a difficult birth often came down to a simple choice: whether to try to save the mother or the baby.

VICTORIAN NURSE c.1865

Sister Mary Benwell

When Mary Benwell told her parents that she wanted to become a nurse, they were horrified: in those days nurses were dirty, illiterate women who often drank too much. But when Mary's father read about Florence Nightingale *(see opposite)* he began to reconsider. After several years he decided that, if Mary was determined to become a nurse, he would allow her to train at one of Miss Nightingale's special schools.

Mary was delighted. She worked hard during her three years' training, attending classes and gaining practical experience in the wards at St Thomas's Hospital in London. She had read Florence Nightingale's book *Notes on Nursing.* It said that care of patients was not only to do with giving medicines and bandaging wounds, but also about making sure that patients were clean and well-looked after. They should be in peaceful surroundings and get regular, nourishing meals.

Mary became one of the first qualified nurses in Britain. She had no wish to get married, much to the concern of her mother, but decided that she would dedicate her whole life to looking after sick people. Although she was not a nun, her sense of vocation was not unlike that of Sister Clare *(see page 8)*.

ABOVE: *Mary's 'chatelaine', which she wore hanging from her belt, had useful items such as scissors and a notebook attached to it.*

CIVIL WAR NURSES

During the American Civil War (1861-65) Dorothea Dix was appointed to be 'Superintendent of the United States Army Nurses'. She insisted that all her nurses be 'plain-looking women' who did not wear fashionable clothes. One of her best nurses was the former slave Harriet Tubman, who had helped many other slaves escape to freedom. Clara Barton, another well-known nurse of the Civil War, was nicknamed the 'Angel of the Battlefield' because she worked on the front line, where the soldiers were actually fighting, rather than in a hospital behind the lines.

ABOVE: *A feeding jug.*
BELOW: *A baby's feeding bottle* (right), *a spout cup feeding bowl for children* (left), *and* (bottom) *a Gibson spoon, which was designed to make sure that patients drank all their medicine. The dose of medicine was poured into the spoon at the top and the lid closed.*
The spoon was placed in the patient's mouth, and the medicine trickled out of a narrow slit at the end.

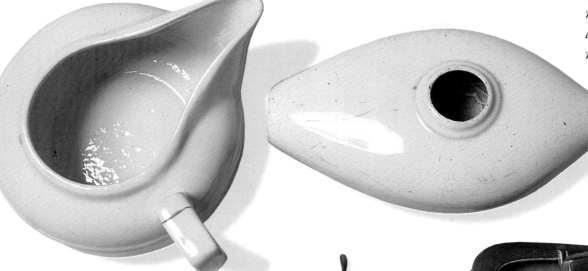

ABOVE: *Florence Nightingale in the Military Hospital at Scutari. Florence (1820-1910) decided to become a nurse against the wishes of her wealthy parents. When Britain went to war against Russia in 1853, she took a small band of nurses out to the Crimea. There she cared for wounded British soldiers who had been poorly looked after by untrained male orderlies in filthy conditions.*

Despite opposition from the military doctors, Florence Nightingale and her nurses cleaned up the rat-infested hospitals and saved many soldiers' lives.

ABOVE: *Ready-made medicines in bottles. As well as giving out medicines, modern nurses receive special training so that they can help during operations.*

VICTORIAN SURGEON c.1870

Charles Pym

Charles Pym first heard about anaesthesia during his medical training in the 1840s. It was said that anaesthetics stopped patients feeling pain during operations. Mr Pym could not believe that such things existed, so he watched an operation using anaesthetics and was amazed to see that the patient was not screaming in agony but lying quite still. Then he wondered whether it was right to use anaesthetics – after all, God made humans suffer pain as a punishment for their wickedness.

An anaesthetic called chloroform was often used to relieve pain during childbirth, and Pym was quite sure that this must be wrong, because the Bible said that women should give birth 'in sorrow', and that meant that they should suffer pain. However, when Queen Victoria was given chloroform during the birth of her eighth child, Leopold, in 1853, Mr Pym changed his mind completely and began to use anaesthetics on his patients. He found that he could do operations that he would have never attempted before. Unfortunately, although Mr Pym's patients did not die from the effects of pain and shock, they often died from infection afterwards, and this worried him.

ABOVE CENTRE:
Surgical scissors.

BELOW: *This stethoscope was invented by a Frenchman, René Laennec, in 1816. Before stethoscopes were invented, the doctor held his ear close to the patient's chest to listen to the sounds made by his or her lungs and heart to help diagnose illness. Modern stethoscopes look very different to this one.*

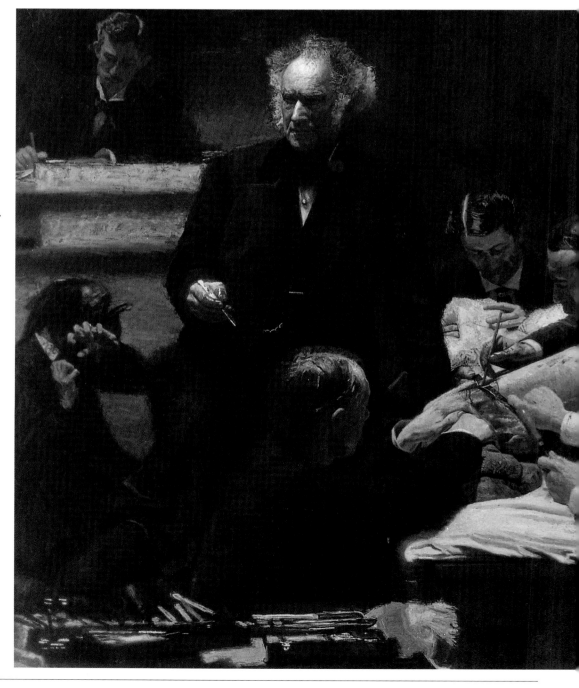

RIGHT: The Gross Clinic, *by Thomas Eakins, 1875. This professor of surgery is operating in his everyday clothes, without a gown, gloves or a mask* (see page 43).

ABOVE: *Mr Pym's surgical instruments. The basic shapes and functions had not changed much since Roman times.*

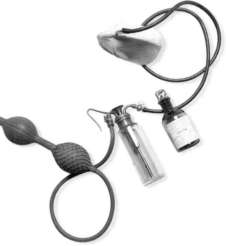

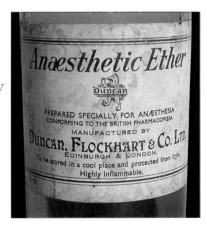

ABOVE: *Chloroform inhalers. The mask was held over the patient's face.*

ANAESTHETICS

There was a gap between the discovery of anaesthesia and its use in surgery. In 1799 Sir Humphry Davy discovered that nitrous oxide could stop people feeling pain, and suggested that it might be used in operations. Instead, it became an attraction at fun fairs, where it was known as 'laughing gas' because it made people giggle. It was not until ether *(right)* was developed by American dentist William Morton in 1846, that anaesthetics became widely used. Chloroform, which was first used in 1847 by British professor James Young Simpson, was also popular. However, because doctors were not experienced in the use of these substances, they sometimes gave their patients too much and killed them. Only at the end of the 19th century could people train to be anaesthetists (see page 42).

Anaesthetic Ether

Duncan

PREPARED SPECIALLY FOR ANÆSTHESIA
CONFORMING TO THE BRITISH PHARMACOPŒIA
MANUFACTURED BY
Duncan, Flockhart & Co. Ltd.
EDINBURGH & LONDON.
To be stored in a cool place and protected from light.
Highly Inflammable.

The general use of anaesthetics had begun in 1846 but the idea of antisepsis (destroying germs) was not widely accepted until the 1870s. This meant that, although patients now underwent pain-free surgery, there was a high risk that they would catch an infection from the dirty conditions in the operating theatre *(see below)*.

This changed when British surgeon Joseph Lister read about Louis Pasteur, a Frenchman who had discovered the existence of germs. Lister realised that germs were causing the infections that killed his patients, so he started to use bandages soaked in a disinfectant called carbolic acid. He also invented a carbolic spray to kill germs during operations *(see opposite)*.

Like many surgeons, Mr Pym did not believe that Lister's methods would work because he did not believe that germs existed. He thought that infection was spread by poisonous mists in the air. But when he saw how many of Lister's patients survived, Mr Pym changed his mind!

ABOVE: *Tourniquet, c.1820. The handle was turned to tighten the strap and prevent blood loss. For how a tourniquet is used, see page 5.*

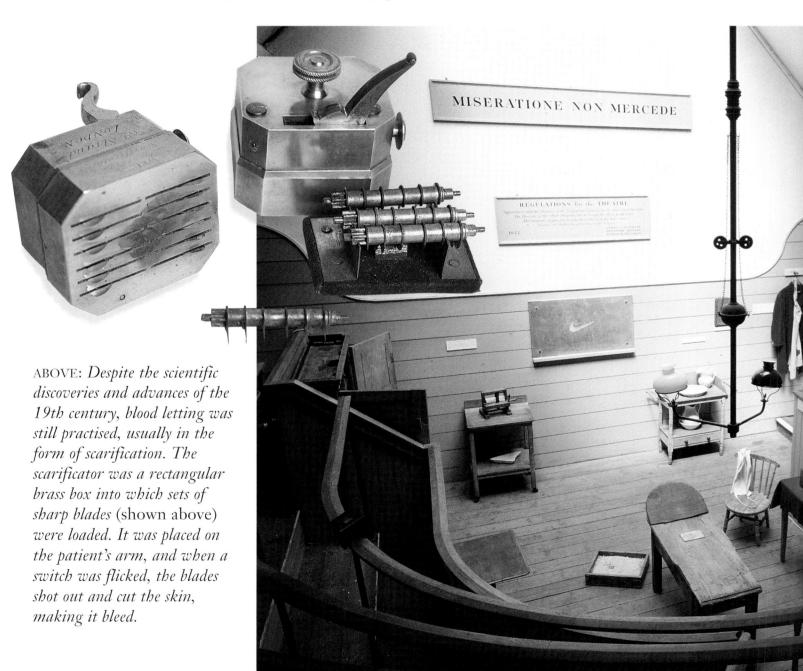

ABOVE: *Despite the scientific discoveries and advances of the 19th century, blood letting was still practised, usually in the form of scarification. The scarificator was a rectangular brass box into which sets of sharp blades (shown above) were loaded. It was placed on the patient's arm, and when a switch was flicked, the blades shot out and cut the skin, making it bleed.*

MISERATIONE NON MERCEDE

LISTER'S CARBOLIC SPRAY

This was first used during operations in 1870. Mr Pym used it to kill germs, but found that it irritated the skin on his hands. This was a problem for many surgeons and their assistants, so in 1890 an American professor of surgery called William Stewart Halstead asked the Goodyear Rubber Company to make him some thin rubber gloves. These were a great success and eventually became standard wear in operating rooms all over the world, along with caps, masks and gowns. Later, asepsis (germ-free conditions) in the operating theatre took the place of antiseptic surgery.

RIGHT: *Thread for sewing up wounds was soaked in carbolic acid to keep it germ-free.*

LEFT: *Operating theatre c.1820. Early operating theatres in hospitals often had tiered rows around a central table, so that medical students could stand and watch the surgeon at work. To the left of the operating table is a wooden box filled with sawdust, which was used to soak up any blood that spilt on the floor. Behind the table on the right is a wash basin. Surgeons washed their hands after operating, but until the discovery of germs they rarely washed their hands before operating. The surgeon's 'operating coat', usually an old frock coat that was stiff with dried blood and pus, is hanging from a hook on the far right. Some surgeons also wore aprons like the ones shown.*

LEFT: *This adjustable 1930s operating table is very different from the one shown far left, which is made of wood and which would be covered by a blanket with a sheet of oil cloth on top to prevent the blood from staining it.*

TROPICAL DOCTOR

Benjamin Cardew

During the 19th century, many European countries colonised other parts of the world, such as Africa. This brought the Europeans into contact with diseases unknown in their home countries. Dr Cardew *(right)*, who arrived in Africa in 1890, was both a missionary and a doctor. His aim was to convert people to Christianity as well as look after their health. However, many of Dr Cardew's patients had diseases such as sleeping sickness, malaria and yellow fever, and they died because he had no way of treating them.

He knew scientists were researching these diseases, and hoped that they would soon find a cure.

ABOVE: *Yellow fever killed many workers during the building of the Panama Canal. In order to prove the theory that the disease was carried by mosquitoes, US soldiers volunteered to be infected.*

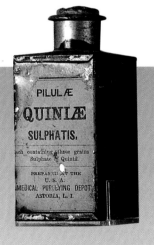

Until 1897, malaria, which gives people attacks of fever and chills, was thought to be caused by bad air. A doctor working in India, named Ronald Ross, discovered that, like yellow fever, malaria was carried by mosquitoes and passed on by their bites.

Dr Cardew used quinine to treat malaria with great success.

GERMS

The greater understanding of what germs did made it easier to identify the cause of tropical diseases and to treat them. Today, people can be vaccinated against many of them, and there are chemical methods of keeping down the mosquito population.

DENTISTRY

In the days before anaesthesia *(see page 26)*, the only treatment for a painful tooth was to pull it out. In medieval times, it was barber-surgeons *(see pages 10-11)* who did this, and many barbers continued to offer tooth extractions as well as hair cuts until at least 1800. It was not until the end of the 19th century that caring for teeth became a profession in its own right, with an examination that had to be passed before anybody could call themselves a dentist. Although anaesthetics meant that pain-free dentistry was available, many people could not afford it. Some young people chose to have all their teeth pulled out and false ones put in to save them trouble and expense in their old age.

Tooth-scrapers have been used to remove scraps of food from between teeth since Roman times. However, toothbrushes did not become widely used until the 19th century, and many people had foul-smelling breath because their teeth were rotting. One reasons why upper-class people used fans was to get rid of the bad smell!

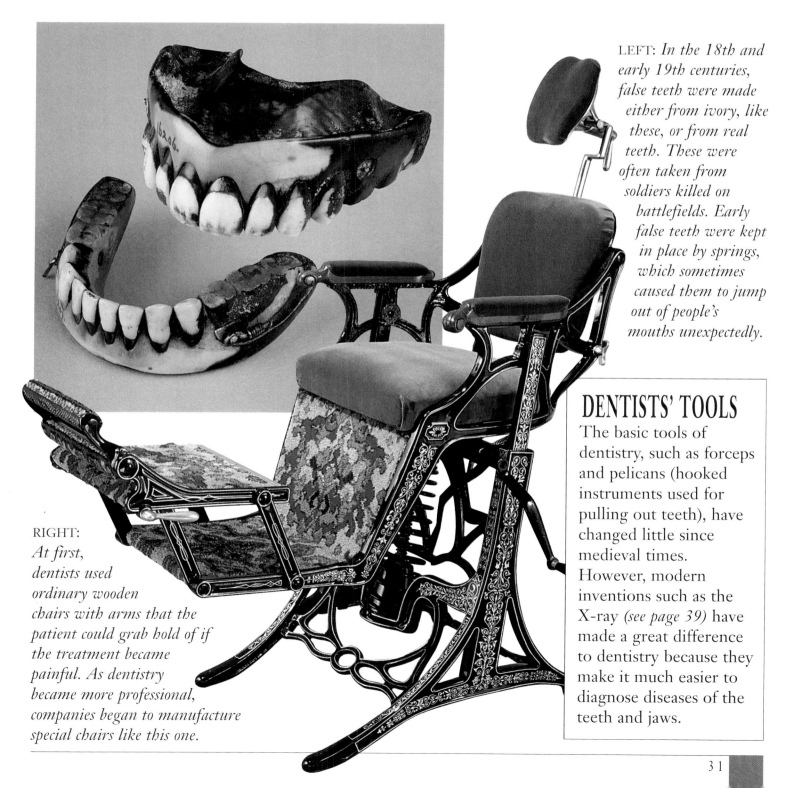

LEFT: *In the 18th and early 19th centuries, false teeth were made either from ivory, like these, or from real teeth. These were often taken from soldiers killed on battlefields. Early false teeth were kept in place by springs, which sometimes caused them to jump out of people's mouths unexpectedly.*

RIGHT: *At first, dentists used ordinary wooden chairs with arms that the patient could grab hold of if the treatment became painful. As dentistry became more professional, companies began to manufacture special chairs like this one.*

DENTISTS' TOOLS

The basic tools of dentistry, such as forceps and pelicans (hooked instruments used for pulling out teeth), have changed little since medieval times. However, modern inventions such as the X-ray *(see page 39)* have made a great difference to dentistry because they make it much easier to diagnose diseases of the teeth and jaws.

FAMILY DOCTOR c.1900

Dr Bernard Covington

After his medical training, Dr Covington decided to go into 'general practice'. This meant that he did not specialise in any particular illness or area of the body, but treated everything. Despite the advances that had been made in medicine, in 1900 infectious diseases such as tuberculosis (TB), which usually affected the lungs and made the sufferer cough up blood, were still killing millions of people.

Dr Covington's black bag contained no medicine to cure TB or vaccination to stop people catching it *(see page 40)*. Instead, he recommended that, if they could afford it, tubercular patients go to a sanitorium, where they would get plenty of fresh air and nourishing food to help their bodies fight off the disease. One disease that Dr Covington was able to treat was diptheria. When he suspected that a child had the disease, he asked her to open her mouth so that he could see if a membrane (thin skin) had grown over the back of her throat, making it hard to breathe. If he saw this, he injected the child with an 'antitoxin' and she soon recovered. Adults who saw this were amazed because, previously, a case of diptheria generally meant death.

As a pain-killer, Dr Covington favoured the aspirin, which had been available for less than a year in 1900. He also recommended laudanum and morphine, which were opiates (taken from opium). Many medicines, including those intended for babies, contained opiates, and several of his patients became addicted to these drugs, which they had bought at the chemist's.

ABOVE CENTRE: *An ear trumpet.*

RIGHT: *Dr Covington's travelling medicine chest.*

ABOVE: *Hypodermic syringe.*

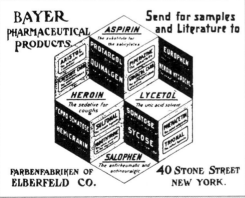

Dr Covington had read about a new drug, heroin, which he thought would be very good for treating his patients. At this time, people did not fully understand that some substances, including opiates such as heroin and morphine, are dangerously addictive.

ABOVE: *Although there were plenty of patent medicines available in 1900, chemists still made up some tablets in their shops, using equipment like this pill-rolling board and capsule-maker.*

HOUSECALLS

Dr Covington's practice was in the country. If he was 'on call' and received a message from a patient to 'come at once', he would travel to that person's house in his pony and trap no matter what time of the day or night it was. A call to go to a remote farmhouse at midnight could involve a very difficult journey. Dr Covington often did not know what he would find when he arrived: it might be an emergency – once or twice, he had performed operations on the kitchen table – or it might be something minor which could really have waited until the following morning.

Housecalls were very tiring and Dr Covington often fell asleep in the trap on the way back.

Fortunately, his pony, Jennifer, knew all the local roads, and she always made sure that he got home safely!

Dr Covington would take a patient's temperature with a thermometer.

FIRST WORLD WAR 1914-18

Sister Elsie Marshall, VAD

By the time the First World War broke out in 1914, Elsie Marshall had been working as a nurse for 10 years. In 1916, she volunteered to nurse the wounded soldiers in France and became a VAD (Voluntary Aid Detachment) nurse. Not all VADs were professional nurses, and Sister Marshall was put in charge of a group of young, inexperienced girls who had had only the most basic training. They worked in a field hospital, about 20 kilometres behind the trenches where the fighting took place.

When a soldier was wounded, he was first picked up from the battlefield on a stretcher and taken to the first-aid post. Then, a horse-drawn ambulance took him to the casualty clearing station, where a doctor from the RAMC (Royal Army Medical Corps) examined him. If the soldier needed immediate treatment, the doctor operated on him and tried to make him as comfortable as possible before he was sent to a field hospital, such as the one where Elsie worked. When the soldier had recovered from his wounds enough to travel, he was sent home to convalesce.

RIGHT: *Stretchers on wheels could be used on bumpy roads, but not on the battlefield, where they would have sunk into the mud and got stuck.*

After a battle was finished, both sides sent stretcher parties out to try to collect wounded soldiers, some of whom might have been lying in water-filled shell-craters for two or three days. If the fighting had been very bad, the stretcher-bearers were ordered to bring back only those men who had a reasonable chance of recovery. On the left is a stretcher-bearer's medical kit.

CENTRE: *Elsie with a soldier who has been blinded in a gas attack* (see below).

RIGHT: *Wheelchairs and crutches were issued to men who had lost the use of their legs or had had them amputated.*

BELOW: *An early X-ray, made on a glass plate, showing shrapnel (the white area) lodged in a soldier's neck.*

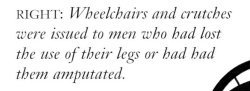

SHELL SHOCK

The fighting in the First World War was different to anything that had been experienced before. Infantrymen attacked the enemy on foot, running towards them across muddy battlefields with rifles and bayonets, just as they had done in the battles of the 19th century. However, the new defences they faced, such as machine-guns and barbed wire, meant that far more men were killed or wounded than in previous wars. The mental strain of this, together with the constant noise of the artillery, sometimes caused shell shock. Some shell-shocked soldiers had panic attacks, others shook all the time, and many were unable to speak or move. At first, the army refused to believe that shell shock existed and said that the men were cowards. By the end of the war there were so many cases that shell shock was recognised officially.

RIGHT: *Gas was used as a weapon by both sides. It blinded soldiers, burned their skin and inflamed their lungs. It also infected wounds, causing gas gangrene. Early gas masks like this one did not give much protection, but by 1917 masks were more effective.*

DISTRICT NURSE c.1930

Sister Margery Gilbert

The job of a district nurse like Sister Margery Gilbert was to travel around a particular area, visiting sick people and looking after them. In the 1930s many women had their babies at home, rather than in hospital. Some district nurses, like Sister Gilbert, were also trained in midwifery, and they helped to deliver these babies. Originally, district nurses were called Queen's Nurses because they were paid for by a fund set up in 1888 in honour of Queen Victoria's Golden Jubilee. District nurses were intended to nurse the poor in their own homes.

Sister Gilbert worked in a poor area of Birmingham. Most of the people she visited lived in homes that were dirty, damp, overcrowded and had no running water or inside toilet. Every day, when she came home from work, Sister Gilbert took off her uniform and shook it over the bath so that the bugs she had picked up on her rounds would fall out.

RIGHT: *Sister Gilbert did her best to help people, but she knew that mothers were not always able to follow her advice about looking after their children. Often, they did not have enough money to buy good food and warm clothes. Sister Gilbert also knew that people would continue to fall ill unless something was done about their poor living conditions.*

TWENTIETH-CENTURY SCIENCE

The amazing advances in medicine in this century are largely due to developments in medical science. One of the most important discoveries that scientists made was how to fight those germs that caused so many deaths from infectious diseases. A German scientist called Paul Ehrlich wanted to develop drugs that would be as effective as the body's own immune system. In 1910 he produced a drug called Salvarsan, which was the first synthetic, or non-natural, drug to fight germs. Later, antibiotics were discovered. These are made in nature and kill germs or prevent them from growing.

BELOW: *Penicillin, the world's first antibiotic, was discovered in 1928 by a bacteriologist called Alexander Fleming. Howard Florey and Ernst Chain developed it by turning the juice of the penicillin mould into a drug that could be used on human beings. By the end of the Second World War, Britain and the United States were producing enough penicillin to treat wounded soldiers.*

ABOVE: *Developed in the 17th century, the microscope made it possible to look at objects too small for the human eye to see. As they became more powerful, microscopes became very important to the study of germs.*

INSULIN

The symptoms of diabetes had been known for years, but the cause was unknown. In 1922 Frederick Banting and Charles Best (*above*) extracted insulin from healthy animals. They knew that people showed the symptoms of diabetes if their bodies could not manufacture insulin, a substance that regulates the level of sugar in the body.

Today, diabetic people have regular injections of insulin to keep them healthy. Modern doctors do not have to taste their patients' urine to find out if they have diabetes (*see page 10*)! Instead they use special testing sticks which change colour when dipped into urine that contains too much sugar.

SECOND WORLD WAR 1939-45

Dr Andrew Duncan and Sister Wendy Nelson

Dr Duncan was working as a surgeon in a London hospital when the Second World War broke out in 1939, and he decided to join the army. Like most doctors who volunteered, he was sent to the Royal Army Medical Corps (RAMC) and made a Captain (all doctors held the rank of officer). He worked in casualty clearing stations *(see page 34)* in many places in Europe, often very close to the fighting. He saved the lives of hundreds of soldiers by performing emergency operations, sometimes in bombed-out homes or in barns, with the patient lying on a kitchen table or on a door which had been taken off its hinges. His assistant was Sister Nelson. Like Sister Marshall *(see page 34)*, she had been a nurse before the war, and volunteered to become a member of the Queen Alexandra Royal Army Nursing Corps (QUARANC). She wore battledress with trousers, rather than the QUARANC nurse's uniform, because it was more suitable for the difficult conditions in which she worked. Doctors and nurses working in the field wore the red cross symbol so that people could identify them as medical staff.

PLASTIC SURGERY

Wounded people in the Second World War benefited from several new medical techniques, one of which was plastic, or 'reconstructive', surgery. During the Battle of Britain in 1940 many fighter pilots, whose planes had caught fire or crashed, suffered horrific burns to their faces and hands. It was discovered that large pieces of skin could be taken from other parts of the patient's body ('donor sites') and attached to the area that had been burnt. Although the new skin did not look completely natural, it was much better than the terrible disfigurement of the burns. The technique has been much improved in the last 50 years.

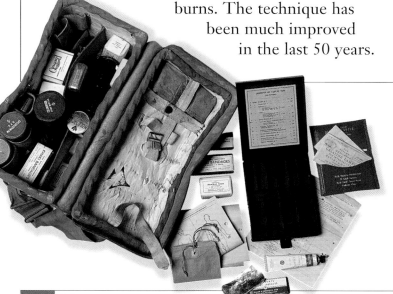

CENTRE: *An emergency operation. Sister Nelson gives the wounded soldier an injection of morphine to deaden the pain. Morphine was supplied in ampoules like the one shown top left. The soldier smokes a cigarette. The dangers of smoking were not known at this time.*
LEFT: *Dr Duncan's field kit.*

MEDICAL ADVANCES

Although there were new and terrible weapons used in both world wars which killed millions of people – in particular the hydrogen bomb in the Second World War – there were also medical advances that saved many lives. In the First World War these included the anti-typhoid vaccine, and in the Second World War the new drug penicillin (see page 37). X-rays and blood transfusions were two other very important advances.

X-rays were discovered in 1895 and were in general use by the time of the Second World War. Doctors could find out exactly where in a wounded soldier's body bullets or pieces of shrapnel had lodged without having to cut him open.

Direct blood transfusions from one person to another had been tried in the 17th century, but it was not until the 1930s that blood could be taken from a donor and stored until needed. Wounded soldiers ran a high risk of dying from blood loss, so it was very important for Dr Duncan and others like him to be able to give blood transfusions. Many civilians gave blood during the war for this purpose.

ABOVE: *Air raid casualty log. For the first time in any war, civilians at home were in just as much danger as soldiers on the battlefield. When bombs were dropped on cities, buildings were often destroyed, leaving wounded people trapped inside. While the rescue services dug them out of the rubble, a 'mobile first-aid post' (a car) with nurses and a doctor waited to examine their injuries. If necessary, people would then be taken to hospital by ambulance.*

GENERAL PRACTITIONER c.1965

Dr Patricia Wilson

Patricia Wilson studied medicine at St Andrew's University in Scotland from 1949 to 1955. Her training included the study of anatomy and physiology *(see page 19)* as well as practical experience. She then had to complete two six-month stints as a junior doctor in a hospital to finish her degree.

She spent the first six months in a casualty department (now called an accident and emergency department), and the second in the department of obstetrics and gynaecology to learn about childbirth and women's illnesses. Patricia was then awarded degrees in medicine and surgery, which meant that she could put the letters MB, ChB after her name. These stand for 'Bachelor of Medicine' and 'Bachelor of Chirurgia' *(see page 10)*.

When her training was complete, Dr Wilson became a GP, or general practitioner, joining an older doctor in a practice in London.

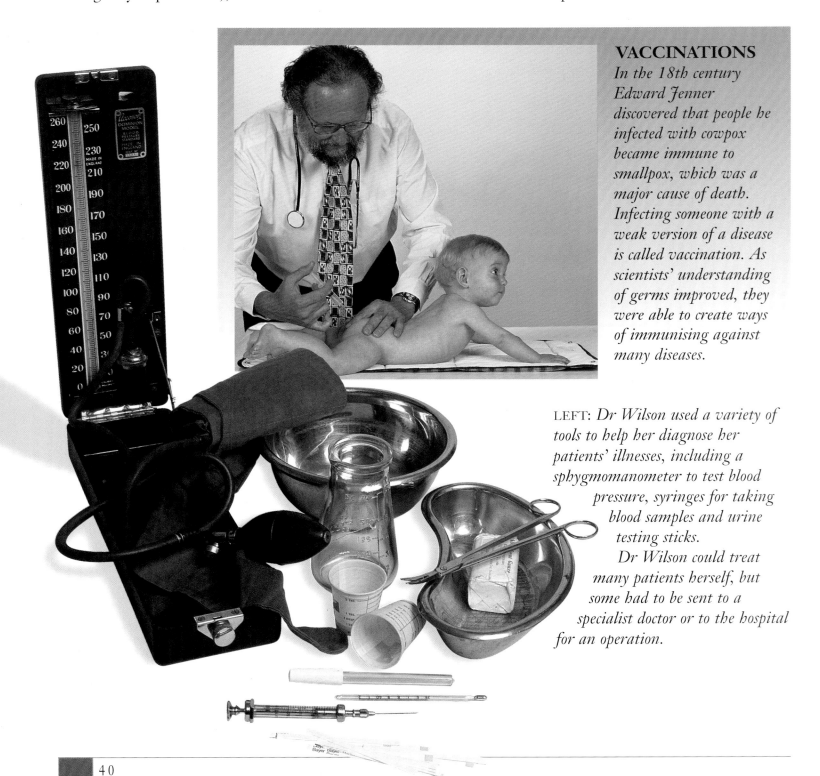

VACCINATIONS

In the 18th century Edward Jenner discovered that people he infected with cowpox became immune to smallpox, which was a major cause of death. Infecting someone with a weak version of a disease is called vaccination. As scientists' understanding of germs improved, they were able to create ways of immunising against many diseases.

LEFT: *Dr Wilson used a variety of tools to help her diagnose her patients' illnesses, including a sphygmomanometer to test blood pressure, syringes for taking blood samples and urine testing sticks.*

Dr Wilson could treat many patients herself, but some had to be sent to a specialist doctor or to the hospital for an operation.

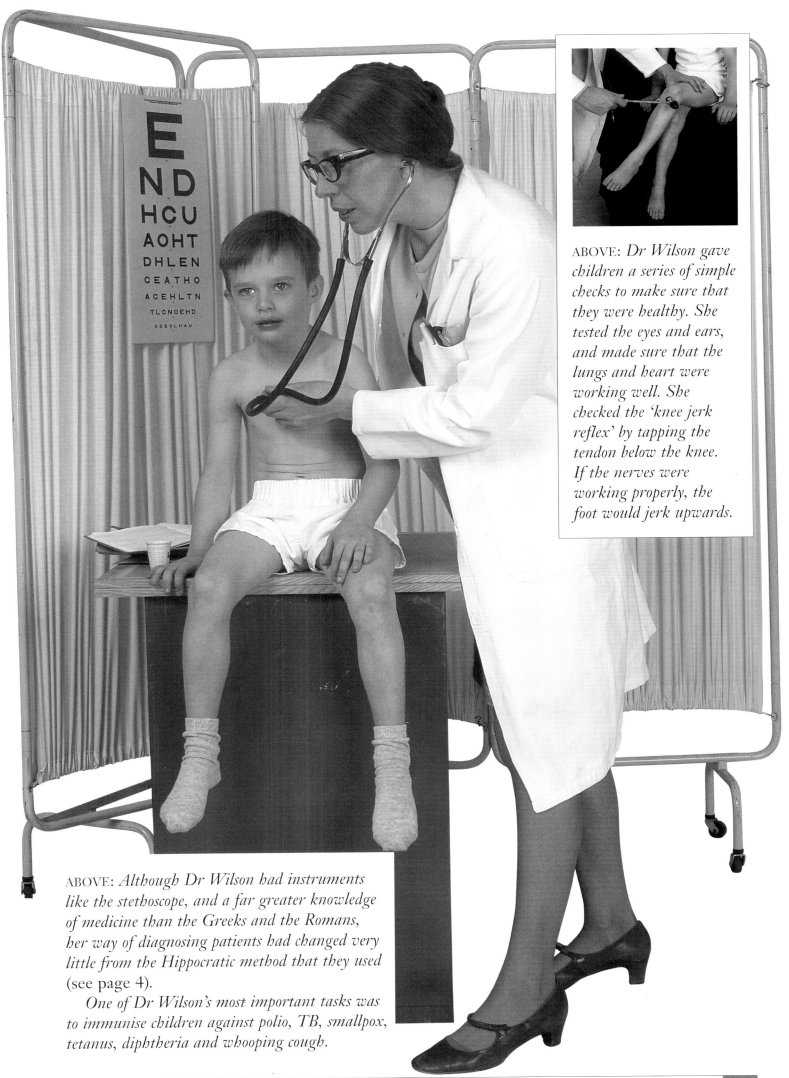

ABOVE: *Dr Wilson gave children a series of simple checks to make sure that they were healthy. She tested the eyes and ears, and made sure that the lungs and heart were working well. She checked the 'knee jerk reflex' by tapping the tendon below the knee. If the nerves were working properly, the foot would jerk upwards.*

ABOVE: *Although Dr Wilson had instruments like the stethoscope, and a far greater knowledge of medicine than the Greeks and the Romans, her way of diagnosing patients had changed very little from the Hippocratic method that they used (see page 4).*

One of Dr Wilson's most important tasks was to immunise children against polio, TB, smallpox, tetanus, diphtheria and whooping cough.

MODERN SURGEON

Mr Alan Wood

Alan Wood qualified as a doctor in 1975 and spent the next 13 years training in surgery. He is now a fully qualified heart and lung specialist and works in a London hospital. Developments in medical science have made a big difference to the diseases that Mr Wood treats. Unlike surgeons working earlier this century, Mr Wood doesn't have to operate on patients with tuberculosis because this disease can be cured with antibiotics. Nor does he have to operate on the valves of the heart as often as he used to; antibiotics can prevent the valves becoming diseased.

Mr Wood often has to operate on people who have heart disease caused by lack of exercise, smoking and eating too much fatty food. He also has many patients suffering from lung cancer because they smoked too many cigarettes.

ABOVE: *Surgical gowns are stored in bags like these.*

RIGHT: *The patient is anaesthetised with intravenous drugs controlled by the equipment at the head of the operating table. The anaesthetist plays a very important role in keeping the patient alive during the operation. He or she will be a fully trained doctor who has gone on to specialise in anaesthesia.*

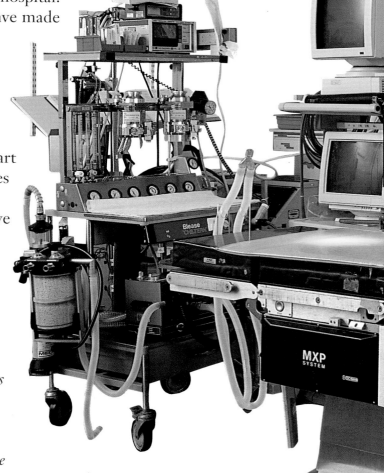

SURGEONS' TOOLS

Surgeons' tools are generally still made of metal, just as they have been for centuries. A lot of instruments are required for heart surgery, and they all have to be sterilised to keep them free of germs. This is done by placing them in a metal tray (*see left*) and heating them in a special machine called an autoclave.

The heart is often stopped during heart surgery, and a machine keeps the blood circulating around the body. When the operation is over, the heart has to be restarted very quickly. These defibrillator paddles (*see right*) are used to deliver electric shocks that will restart the stopped heart.

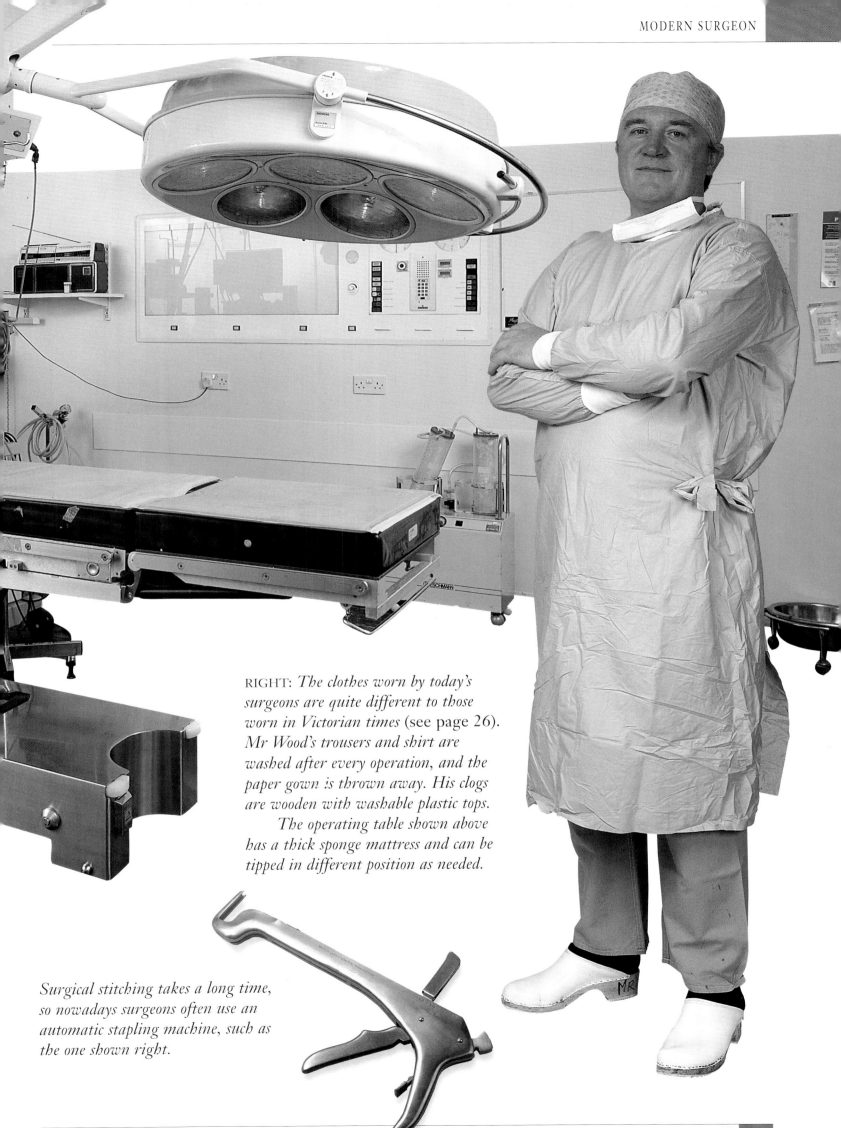

RIGHT: *The clothes worn by today's surgeons are quite different to those worn in Victorian times (see page 26). Mr Wood's trousers and shirt are washed after every operation, and the paper gown is thrown away. His clogs are wooden with washable plastic tops.*

The operating table shown above has a thick sponge mattress and can be tipped in different position as needed.

Surgical stitching takes a long time, so nowadays surgeons often use an automatic stapling machine, such as the one shown right.

LEFT: *Lucius Spectatus's medical instruments.*

RIGHT: *American Indian medicine bundles.*

TIME LINE

*c.*10,000 BC • Prehistoric people practise 'trepanation'. In this operation, a hole is bored into the patient's skull with sharpened stone tools in the belief that it will allow 'evil spirits' to escape.

*c.*420 BC • Hippocrates is teaching medicine on Kos, an island in Greece.

129 AD • Galen is born in Pergamum, part of the Roman Empire. He later studied in Egypt and in Italy.

*c.*500 • The Fall of the Roman Empire leads to a loss of ancient medical knowledge.

1123 • St Bartholomew's Hospital is founded in London.

*c.*1250 • The first Islamic medical schools are opened in Turkey.

*c.*1315 • The first recorded dissection of a human body is performed by Mondino dei Liuzzi in Bologna, Italy.

1347 • The Black Death begins in Europe.

1543 • *De Humani Corporis Fabrica* ('The Fabric of the Human Body') is produced by Andreas Vesalius. This was the first collection of accurate anatomical drawings.

1628 • William Harvey writes about the way blood circulates round the body.

1665 • The Great Plague devastates London.

1714 • Gabriel Daniel Fahrenheit invents the mercury thermometer.

1796 • The first vaccination against smallpox is given by Edward Jenner.

Plague doctor John Watson.

1799 • Sir Humphry Davy discovers that nitrous oxide eases pain.

1816 • René Laennec invents the stethoscope.

1817 • The first cholera epidemic begins.

1840 • The Institute of Nursing is founded in London by Elizabeth Fry.

1844 • Horace Wells uses nitrous oxide to extract one of his own teeth.

1846 • William Thomas Morton, an American dentist, uses ether as an anaesthetic.

1847 • James Young Simpson uses chloroform to relieve the pain of childbirth.

1853 • Smallpox vaccinations become compulsory in England.

1860 • Florence Nightingale's Nursing School is opened at St Thomas's Hospital, London.

1861 • Louis Pasteur discovers how bacteria work.

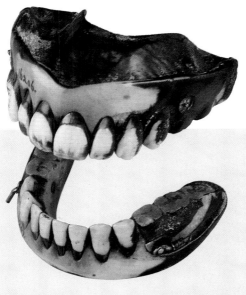

False teeth made from ivory.

1865 • Joseph Lister begins using disinfectants in surgery.

1885 • Louis Pasteur develops a vaccine for rabies.

1890 • William Stewart Halstead invents surgical gloves.

1893 • In America, Daniel Williams performs the first open-heart surgery.

1895 • Wilhelm Roentgen discovers 'X-rays'.

1897 • Ronald Ross discovers that malaria is carried by mosquitoes.

1899 • Aspirin goes on sale.

1905 • George Washington Crile performs the first direct blood transfusion.

1910 • Paul Ehrlich develops Salvarsan, a cure for syphilis, and becomes a pioneer in chemotherapy.

1918–19 • An influenza pandemic rages across the world, killing between 15 and 25 million people, more than died in the First World War itself.

1922 • Frederick Banting and Charles Best isolate insulin.

1928 • Alexander Fleming discovers penicillin.

1935 • The first blood bank is opened in America.

1937 • The yellow fever vaccine is developed by Max Theiler.

1940 • Howard Florey and Ernst Chain develop penicillin as an antibiotic.

1945 • Fluoride is added to the American water supply to reduce tooth decay.

1952 • Artificial heart valves are used in open-heart surgery.

1957 • A live polio vaccine is developed by Albert Sabin.

1967 • Christiaan Barnard performs the first successful human heart transplant.

1978 • The first "test-tube" baby is born in England.

1979 • Smallpox is declared eradicated from the world.

1981 • AIDS is first recognized by U.S. Centers for Disease Control.

1980s • Surgeons begin using less 'invasive' methods, such as keyhole surgery in which viewing tubes called endoscopes are inserted into the body.

1987 • The pencil laser is invented in France. Laser beams can be used instead of scalpels, causing the patient less damage or 'trauma'.

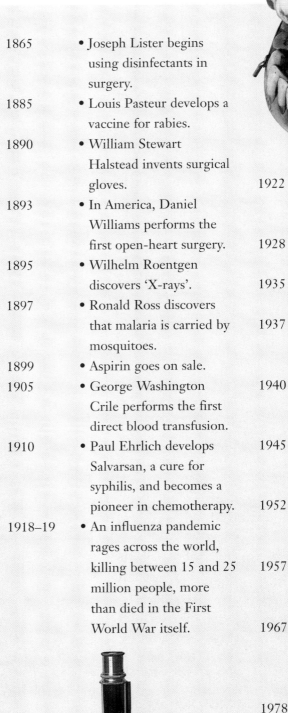

An early microscope

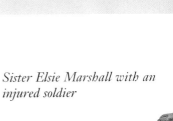

Sister Elsie Marshall with an injured soldier

GLOSSARY

Amputate To cut off an injured limb, which might otherwise become infected and cause death.

Anaesthesia Putting a patient to sleep while a surgeon performs an operation. The anaesthetist does this either by injections, or by having the patient breathe in an anaesthetic gas.

Antisepsis Applying suitable substances (antiseptics) to wounds and injuries to kill germs. *See also* asepsis.

Antitoxin A substance used to counteract poisons (toxins).

Asepsis Keeping an area – an operating theatre for example – totally free of germs. *See also* antisepsis.

Bacteria These are tiny organisms living in soil, air and water, which can cause disease in humans.

Cataract An opaque spot that can grow on the lens of the eye, causing a gradual worsening of vision.

Comfits Sweets or pastilles made with fruits or roots, preserved in sugar.

Constipation Difficulty in emptying the bowels (going to the toilet), or not being able to do so for a longer than normal time. This can happen particularly in illness, or after an operation. *See also* laxative and purgative.

Contagious Describes a disease that can be passed from one person to another by touch only.

Diabetes A protein called insulin controls the way in which the body deals with sugar levels in the blood. People who suffer from diabetes do not have enough insulin in their system, so that blood sugar quantities increase too much, and excess urine is produced. Nowadays diabetics are generally able to control the disorder through injections of insulin.

Diuretic Describes a drug that helps people to urinate, and which is necessary in the treatment of certain disorders: for example, high blood pressure.

Drug Any substance that can be used medically in the treatment of disease. Those drugs that bring drowsiness and sleep – derived from opium and morphine – are used as pain-killers.

Emetic A medicine that is used to make people vomit.

Forceps An instrument, like a pair of pincers, used in surgery and dentistry.

Gangrene An injured toe, leg, foot, or other part of the body, can be deprived of its blood supply, become infected by bacteria, and the body tissue around the wound can die. Amputation of a gangrenous limb may be necessary in the worst cases.

Haemorrhoids Also called piles. Painful, swollen veins in the anus.

Hernia An organ inside the body which moves out of place, and pushes through the wall of the cavity which normally contains it.

Immunity Being immune to a disease is being able to resist it. Some people have a natural resistance to infection, others are less lucky. It is possible for the body to gain immunity to infections that previously attacked it because antibodies produced in the blood fight off further attack. Sometimes it is sensitised body cells that keep out repeat infection.

Infectious Describes a disease that can be passed from one person to another.

Infirmary A hospital.

Laxative A drug which causes the bowels to empty. *See also* constipation and purgative.

Medicine The scientific study of human illnesses, how they are caused, prevented and treated.

Opiates From opium; drugs that bring about drowsiness or sleep.

Patent medicines The owner of a patent was allowed to produce and sell his medicine under his own brand name – no one else could copy the recipe or the name. Sometimes the brand name became a household name. Sometimes such medicines were sold as having magic ingredients. This is forbidden by law today. Each medicine must be labelled with what it contains.

Pneumonia A disease of the lungs, which become inflamed and cause shortness of breath and serious illness. Pneumonic plague attacked Londoners during the Great Plague.

Poultices These were applied to the skin to help soothe soreness or inflammation. They were made by pouring boiling water on to a soft substance such as bread, then wrapping the mash in muslin or linen to put on the affected part.

Purgative A drug that causes the bowels to empty. *See also* constipation and laxative.

Pus A yellowish liquid that can appear on the surface of an inflamed wound.

Red Cross An international organisation formed in 1864 to give help to the wounded and prisoners of war. The modern Red Cross is active world-wide whenever there is distress or need. The symbol of a red cross on a white background originates with the Crusaders.

Resurrection Rising from the dead.

Salve To treat a cut or other wound with a soothing ointment or dressing. The word also applies to the ointment itself.

Shock Serious bleeding after an accident or traumatic event can put a person in shock. Blood pressure decreases and the brain cannot work normally. People also use the word in a more general way to describe the grief or fear that might affect them following such an event.

INDEX

PLACES TO VISIT

Alexander Fleming Laboratory Museum
St Mary's Hospital
Praed Street
London W2 1NY
Tel: 0171 725 6528

Balfour Museum of Hampshire
Red Cross History
Red Cross House
Stockbridge Road
Weeke
Winchester
Hampshire SO22 5JD
Tel: 01962 865174

British Dental Association Museum
64 Wimpole Street
London, W1M 8AL
Tel: 0171 935 0875

Cookworthy Museum of Rural Life
in South Devon
108 Fore Street
Kingsbridge
South Devon TQ7 1AW
Tel: 01548 853235

Dental Hospital Museum
School of Dental Surgery
Liverpool University
Edwards Building
Pembroke Place
Liverpool L3 5PS
Tel: 0151 794 2000

Freud Museum
20 Maresfield Gardens
Hampstead
London NW3 5SX
Tel: 0171 435 2002

Hall's Croft
c/o The Shakespeare Birthplace Trust·
Old Town
Stratford Upon Avon CV37 6BG
Tel: 01789 292107

Hitchin Museum & Art Gallery
Paynes Park
Hitchin
Hertfordshire SG5 1EQ
Tel: 01462 434476

Museum of Childhood
42 High Street (Royal Mile)
Edinburgh
Scotland EH1 1TG
Tel: 0131 529 4142

Museum of The History of Science
Broad Street
Oxford
Oxfordshire OX1 3AZ
Tel: 01865 277280/815559

Museum of The Order of St John
St John's Gate
St John's Lane
Clerkenwell
London EC1M 4DA
Tel: 0171 253 6644

Museum of The Royal College of Surgeons
of Edinburgh
Nicolson Street
Edinburgh
Scotland EH8 9DW
Tel: 0131 527 1600

Museum of The Royal Pharmaceutical
Society of Great Britain
1 Lambeth High Street
London SE1 7JN
Tel: 0171 735 9141

Royal Museum of Scotland
Chambers Street
Edinburgh
Scotland EH1 1JF
Tel: 0131 225 7534

Science Museum
Exhibition Road
South Kensington
London SW7 2DD
Tel: 0171 938 8000

Staffordshire County Museum
Shugborough Estate
Milford
Nr Stafford
Staffordshire ST17 0XB
Tel: 01889 881388

Sunnyside Museum
Sunnyside Royal Hospital
Hillside
Montrose
Scotland DD109JP
Tel: 01674 830361

Thirsk Museum
14-16 Kirkgate
Thirsk
North Yorkshire YO7 1PQ
Tel: 01845 522755
(c/o Thirsk Tourist Information Office)

The Wellcome Trust
The Wellcome Building
183 Euston Road
London NW1 2BE
Tel: 0171 611 8888/7211

ACKNOWLEDGEMENTS

Breslich & Foss would like to thank the following people and organisations for sharing their expertise and enthusiasm with us, for allowing themselves to be photographed, for lending us equipment and for answering our questions so patiently:

pp4–5 Ian Post of Roman Military Research.

pp6–7 John Cole, David Page and Ian Jeremiah of Conquest.

pp8–9 Don Holton and Kathryn Williams of Heuristics; leeches supplied by Biopharm.

pp10–11 Victor Shreeve and Simon Metcalf.

pp12–13 Jon Price and Karl Watkiss of Time Travellers.

pp14–15 Ruth Goodman, Mark Griffin of Griffin Historical.

pp16–17 Stephen Wisdom.

pp18–19 Stephen Wisdom.

pp20–21 Henry Real Bird, Michael Terry (Native American Consultant and supplier of clothing and regalia).

pp22–23 Jacqueline Hale of Time Travellers.

pp24–25 Wendy Morris.

pp26–27 Jon Price of Time Travellers.

pp28–29 The Old Operating Theatre, Museum and Herb Garret, by kind permission of the Chapter House Group.

pp30–31 Keith Major.

pp32–33 Rob Thrush.

pp34–35 Christine Hunt, Keith Major.

pp36–37 Lynette Brayley.

pp38–39 Richard Ingram, Susannah Whitehouse, Martin Brayley.

pp40–41 Janet Ravenscroft, Alexander Osborne, Dr Elizabeth Storring and Dr June Wilson.

pp42–43 Alan Wood, photographed at the London Independent Hospital.

Breslich & Foss would also like to thank Nick Hall and Richard Ingram of Sabre Sales, 85 Castle Road, Southsea, Hants, and Captain Peter Starling of the Royal Army Medical Corps Museum for the use of clothing and artefacts; Angels & Bermans for costumes on pp24–25 and 40–41; STV for artefacts on pp32–33 and 40–41.

With thanks to my secretary, Priscilla Mahmut, for typing the text, and to my daughter Nicola for her invaluable assistance.
Rod Storring

Picture credits:
AKG Photo, London p30, top right. Bridgeman Art Library p26, centre. E.T. archive p17, top right; p25, top. Hulton Getty p37, bottom left. Mary Evans Picture Library p19, right; p22, centre. Science Museum/Science & Society Picture Library p31, both; p37, centre; /NMPFT p37, right; /CC studio p40, centre. Museum of London pp16–17. Wellcome Centre for Medical Science p18, bottom right.

MASTERS OF ART

VAN GOGH

Enrica Crispino

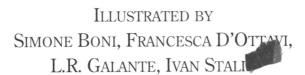

Illustrated by
Simone Boni, Francesca D'Ottavi,
L.R. Galante, Ivan Stali

Macdonald Young Books

DoGi

Produced by
Donati Giudici Associati, Florence
Original title:
*Van Gogh, l'esperienza straordinaria
del colore*
Text:
Enrica Crispino
Illustrations:
*Simone Boni, Francesca D'Ottavi,
L.R. Galante, Ivan Stalio*
Picture research and coordination of
co-editions:
Caroline Godard
Art direction:
*Oliviero Ciriaci
Sebastiano Ranchetti
Alessandro Rabatti*
Page design:
Sebastiano Ranchetti
Editing:
Enza Fontana
English translation:
Deborah Misuri-Charkham
Editor, English-language edition:
Ruth Nason
Typesetting:
Ken Alston – A.J. Latham Ltd

© 1996 Donati Giudici Associati s.r.l.
Florence, Italy

English language text © 1996 by
Macdonald Young Books/
Peter Bedrick Books
First published in Great Britain
in 1996 by
Macdonald Young Books
61 Western Road
Hove
East Sussex BN3 1JD

Printed in 1996 by Amilcare Pizzi,
Cinisello Balsamo (Milan)

Photolitho:
Venanzoni DTP, Florence

♦ HOW THE INFORMATION IS PRESENTED

Every double-page spread is a chapter in its own right, devoted to an aspect of the life and art of Vincent van Gogh or the major artistic and cultural developments of his time. The text at the top of the left-hand page (1) and the large central illustration are concerned with this main theme. The text in italics (2) gives a chronological account of events in van Gogh's life. The other material (photographs, paintings and drawings) enlarges on the central theme.

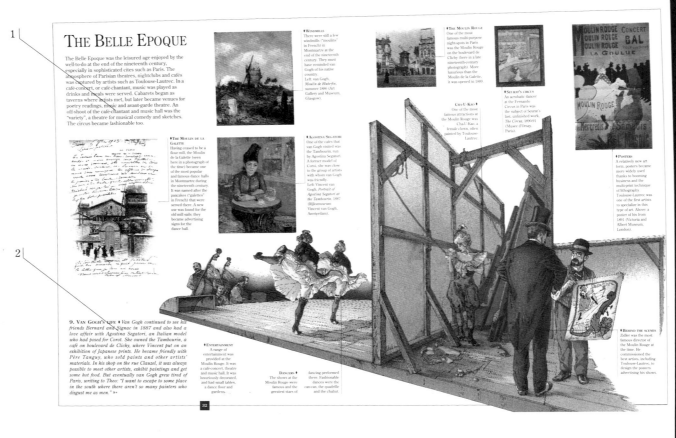

THE BELLE EPOQUE

The Belle Epoque was the leisured age enjoyed by the well-to-do at the end of the nineteenth century, especially in sophisticated cities such as Paris. The atmosphere of Parisian theatres, nightclubs and cafés was captured by artists such as Toulouse-Lautrec. In a café-concert, or café-chantant, music was played as drinks and meals were served. Cabarets began as taverns where artists met, but later became venues for poetry readings, music and avant-garde theatre. An off-shoot of the café-chantant and music hall was the "variety", a theatre for musical comedy and sketches. The circus became fashionable too.

Some pages focus on major works by van Gogh. They include the following information: an account of the painting's history (1); a description of the content and imagery of the work (2); a critical analysis and detailed examination of its formal aspects (3). There are also reproductions of works by other artists, to set van Gogh's work in its historical context and demonstrate its originality.

BEDROOM IN ARLES

Van Gogh described this painting of his bedroom in the Yellow House, in a letter of 1888: "It is just simply my bedroom ... The walls are pale violet. The floor is covered with red tiles, the wooden bedhead and chairs are as yellow as fresh butter, the sheets and pillows are very pale lemon green. The blanket is scarlet. The window green. The wash-stand is orange and the basin blue. The doors are lilac ... There are some paintings on the wall, a towel and some clothes."

CONTENTS

CONTEMPORARIES

Vincent van Gogh's life was brief and tormented. He could never achieve peace of mind and his relationships always failed. People who came into close contact with him found it hard to cope with his moods and strange behaviour. This was the case even for those who most loved and admired him, such as his brother Theo and fellow artists Bernard and Gauguin. Yet, today, van Gogh is perhaps the most admired artist in the world. His paintings fetch the highest prices and exhibitions of his works attract record numbers of visitors. Without doubt, van Gogh was one of the greatest and most innovative artists of the late nineteenth century: his many masterpieces, from *Bedroom in Arles* to *Starry Night*, are evidence of this. One of the new ideas that he introduced, which has most affected modern art, was that painting could express the feelings and inner world of the artist, rather than being an objective representation of the outside world. Van Gogh had links with all the original trends in art of his time, from Realism to Impressionism, from Seurat's Neo-Impressionism to the Synthetism of Bernard and Gauguin and the Expressionist movement, of which he has often been seen as a forerunner.

♦ JULIEN TANGUY
(1825-1894)
Père Tanguy, as his friends called him, had a shop in Paris selling paints. Artists of van Gogh's generation bought their materials from him.

♦ EMILE BERNARD
(1868-1941)
This French painter and important art theorist was one of the first people to recognize van Gogh's talent. He remained a lifelong faithful friend.

CAMILLE PISSARRO ♦
(1830-1903)
One of the chief French Impressionists, Pissarro later also painted in the divisionist style. He and his son Lucien were friends of Theo and Vincent van Gogh. He introduced Vincent to Dr Gachet.

♦ JEAN-FRANÇOIS MILLET
(1814-1875)
Millet was a master of French realistic painting. His scenes of peasant life were one of van Gogh's artistic models.

♦ GEORGES SEURAT
(1859-1891)
The pioneer of divisionism, one of the great innovations in French painting, Seurat was a master whom van Gogh greatly admired.

VINCENT VAN GOGH ♦
(1853-1890)
Van Gogh's appearance is familiar to us because of his many self-portraits: red hair, often a short beard, bright and expressive eyes.

♦ PAUL GAUGUIN
(1848-1903)
Gauguin introduced a bold new decorative style of painting in the late nineteenth century. He moved from France to live in Polynesia.

HENRI DE ♦ TOULOUSE-LAUTREC
(1864-1901)
Paris nightlife was the subject of Lautrec's paintings. Two falls in his youth had stopped his legs from growing.

THEO VAN GOGH ♦
(1857-1891)
Theo was Vincent's favourite brother. He tried to help him in any way he could, and it was to him that Vincent wrote most of his letters. Theo was an art dealer. He married and had a son named after Vincent.

SIEN ♦
Clasina Maria Hoornik, known as Sien, was a prostitute in The Hague with whom van Gogh became involved. He took her to live with him, partly out of a feeling that she had been abandoned and needed someone to look after her, but the relationship ended after a year or so.

♦JOSEPH ROULIN
A postal worker in Arles, Roulin was cheerful and unconventional and loved wine and became one of van Gogh's few real friends.

MARIE GINOUX ♦
Marie was the wife of Joseph Ginoux, who owned the café that van Gogh went to in Arles. She is the subject of a famous painting by van Gogh.

MINERS ♦
Van Gogh spent from 1878 to 1880 in the Belgian coalmining area of the Borinage. He went there as a preacher and devoted himself to alleviating the suffering of the miners, whose working and living conditions were appalling, and sharing their daily hardships.

PARENTS ♦
Van Gogh's father, Theodorus (1822-1885), was a Protestant minister. His mother, Anna Cornelia (1819-1907), was the daughter of a bookbinder in The Hague.

DOCTOR GACHET ♦
(1828-1909)
Paul-Ferdinand Gachet often invited van Gogh to his house in Auvers, near Paris, and helped him as a doctor in the last months of his life. He was friendly with artists such as Pissarro and Cézanne and himself painted as a hobby.

GROOT ZUNDERT

At the end of the nineteenth century, the inland regions of Holland remained untouched by the cultural interests, lively, tolerant atmosphere and openness to trade that had characterized Dutch coastal cities for centuries. It was in one of these inland regions, the province of Brabant, that Vincent van Gogh was born, son and grandson of Protestant clergymen. His background ensured that he came to hold deep religious beliefs, which lasted all his life, even though he became disillusioned and left the Church. There was, however, another family interest which, for Vincent, would become a passion: painting. Three of his uncles were art dealers and one of his mother's relations, Anton Mauve, was a leader of The Hague School of painting.

♦ BRABANT

In the nineteenth century the Dutch province of Brabant, on the country's border with Belgium, was predominantly agricultural. Its inhabitants were a mix of Catholics and Protestants. The region remained relatively backward at a time when Holland's industry was expanding and trade with the colonies in the East Indies was growing.

VINCENT'S PARENTS ♦

Theodorus van Gogh was the son of a Protestant pastor and became a pastor himself. He settled in the parish of Groot Zundert in 1849. Two years later, he married Anna Cornelia Carbentus. The couple's first child was still-born. Then Vincent was born and after him five others.

VAN GOGH'S LIFE

1. *Vincent's father, Theodorus van Gogh, was the Protestant pastor of Groot Zundert, a rural village in the province of Brabant, some 80 kilometres (50 miles) from Breda, in southern Holland. His mother, Anna Cornelia Carbentus, was the daughter of a bookbinder at the court of The Hague. Vincent was born on 30 March 1853, in the house next to the church at Zundert, and exactly one year after his older brother, also named Vincent, had died at birth. The next son, Theodorus, known as Theo, was born on 1 May 1857 and Vincent became very attached to him from the start. Vincent went to boarding school, near Zundert, but family finances soon made it necessary for him to leave and find a job.* ⮕

LONDON

The 1870s, for Great Britain, were years marked by efforts to expand its empire to include Egypt, Afghanistan and South Africa. Queen Victoria became Empress of India in 1876, by which time the British Empire, protected by the Royal Navy, covered vast areas of the world. Rapid industrial development was also taking place, and so Britain was seen as the "workshop of the world". The other side of the coin was that millions of British working people were living at subsistence level, in poor and degrading conditions. In the poverty-stricken districts of London, hundreds of thousands of malnourished men, women and children were crowded into appallingly unhygienic accommodation. This was the London that Charles Dickens described in his novels. For some years, radical and Christian philanthropists had agitated to improve the conditions of the poor. Van Gogh came into contact with such people during his stay in England from 1873 to 1875.

♦ **THE BRITISH EMPIRE** During the last decades of the nineteenth century, the British Empire was by far the largest of all the empires built by European powers.

Great Britain

British Empire

♦ **QUEEN VICTORIA** (1819-1901) The niece of William IV, Victoria succeeded him to the British throne in 1837 and remained Queen until her death. She was a forthright character, who gave her name to the long period of British history known as the Victorian Age. Left: *Portrait of Queen Victoria* by Edward M. Ward (Forbes Magazine Collection, New York).

MEANS OF ♦ TRANSPORT At the end of the nineteenth century in London, goods were still transported by horse-drawn carts, while people needing to travel around could use the underground or electric trams. Motor vehicles did not become widespread, because, until 1896, English law set the speed limit at 6 kilometres (4 miles) per hour.

♦ WORKERS
Living conditions of workers were extremely poor and trade unionists began to agitate to demand more humane working hours and better working conditions in the factories.

♦ POVERTY
Britain's rich-poor divide was particularly obvious in London. In this richest city in the world, thousands of people suffered from malnutrition and lived in unhealthy dwellings.

♦ FROM ENGLAND
Vincent's letters to Theo are a mine of information about his life. In one dated April 1876, he included this sketch of Ramsgate, on the southeast coast of England (Rijks- museum Vincent van Gogh, Amsterdam). Vincent moved there after a few months' work in Paris.

♦ MYSTERY IN FACT AND FICTION
Between the summer and the start of winter in 1888, London was shocked by a series of savage murders. In some cases the murderer wrote a letter to the newspapers, saying when he would strike next. In total there were six victims of Jack the Ripper. Mysteries reigned in literature, too: in 1887, Arthur Conan Doyle began to write stories about Sherlock Holmes (right in this drawing), king of fictional detectives.

2. VAN GOGH'S LIFE ♦ *Van Gogh's Uncle Vincent was a partner in a firm of art dealers, Goupil and Co., whose head office was in Paris. In summer 1869 he found his nephew a job in Goupil's branch in The Hague and in 1873 Theo also joined Goupil's, in Brussels. Also in 1873, Vincent visited Paris for the first time, for a few days, and then went on to the London office. As he gained experience, his interest in art began to grow, and his job allowed him to broaden his knowledge. In London he would take long walks and make sketches of the city. He left his first accommodation, which was too expensive, to lodge with Mrs Loyer, a clergyman's widow. Soon he fell in love with her daughter, Eugénie, who was already engaged and firmly rejected him. Vincent became extremely downhearted, suffered from loneliness and increasingly turned to religion for consolation. He read the Bible zealously and often went to church.* ➤

REALISM

Between 1830 and 1860, in France, Realism became important in literature and in painting. Writers and artists in this new style took their subjects from everyday life, describing them realistically. Because of the progress that had been made in technology and medicine, people put great faith in science. Thinkers of the time put forward socialist ideas and positivist philosophies, the basis of which was that all meaningful knowledge came from what could be seen and experienced. The painters who turned towards Realism were rebelling against the art academies and against the belief that the most important art was that which represented historical and mythological subjects. The Barbizon School painted real landscapes, and artists such as Courbet and Millet portrayed ordinary people. Such paintings of people at work and simple woodland scenes were not easy for traditionalists to accept. But van Gogh had no doubts. He liked to paint peasant life and the artist he modelled himself on at first was Millet.

♦ **EMILE ZOLA AND NATURALISM**
The French novelist Emile Zola (1840-1902) led the Naturalist movement, which held that literature should describe life from an objective viewpoint, in "scientific" detail. He claimed that he put characters in a particular social setting and then studied the interaction between their temperament and the environment. Left: *Emile Zola*, by Manet, 1868, detail (Musée d'Orsay, Paris).

♦ **WOODLAND** ♦ 1
During the 1830s a group of landscape painters settled in the village of Barbizon, on the edge of the Forest of Fontainebleau. Woods and trees were the favourite subjects of Théodore Rousseau, Charles Daubigny and Jean-François Millet.
1.2.3. Gustave Courbet, *The Vercingetorix Oak*, 1864, details and complete (Pennsylvania Academy of Fine Arts, Philadelphia); 4. Théodore Rousseau, *Morning in the Forest of Fontainebleau*, 1850 (Wallace Collection, London); 5. Jean-François Millet, *Spring*, 1868-73 (Musée d'Orsay, Paris).

♦ **A SHOCKING PAINTING**
Gustave Courbet (1819-1877) became the leader of the Realist movement in art.

His painting *Burial at Ornans*, 1849-50 (Musée d'Orsay, Paris), was exhibited at the Salon of 1850-51 and caused an uproar.

Never before had a scene with working people been presented in this way. Courbet had established a new kind of social art.

♦ **ANIMALS** ♦ 1
Rejecting the Romantic style of the earlier nineteenth century, the Realist painters, whether they belonged to the Barbizon School or followed Gustave Courbet, were interested in any subject taken from the natural world, including animals.
1. Constant Troyon, *The Pointer*, 1860 (Museum of Fine Arts, Boston); 2. Gustave Courbet, *Spring Mating Season*, 1861 (Musée d'Orsay, Paris).

3. VAN GOGH'S LIFE ♦ *In a letter to Theo in January 1874, Vincent listed his favourite painters. He mentioned fifty-six, including Millet, Rousseau, Breton, Troyon and Mauve – all exponents of Realism. In 1875, he was transferred to Goupil's head office in Paris but seems to have neglected his duties as he became more and more deeply religious. On 1 April 1876 he was dismissed. He then returned to England, where he worked as a teacher, first in Ramsgate and then in the London suburb of Isleworth. Here, the headmaster, the Reverend Jones, also employed him as an assistant in his church. In December van Gogh returned to his parents' home: they had moved to the village of Etten, near Breda. In 1877 he started work in a Dordrecht bookshop but left for Amsterdam in May. His plans to study theology at the university there came to nothing.* ⇒

THE MINES

In the second half of the nineteenth century, Belgium was one of the world's largest producers of coal. The coalmines were the source of the country's wealth, thanks to advances in technology which had made it possible to increase production. The introduction of wheeled carts for transporting coal along underground tracks and steam-driven elevators for lifting it to the surface had somewhat improved working conditions in the mines, but, even so, a collier's life was still extremely hard. Van Gogh went as a lay preacher to the Belgian mining region of the Borinage, where he felt driven to share the miners' experience of life. Men, women and children were forced to perform backbreaking tasks, in an unhealthy atmosphere where safety precautions were almost non-existent. They were paid a pittance and lived in squalid conditions.

♦ THE MINERS
The miners' poor living conditions were almost the only subject that van Gogh drew and painted when he was in the Borinage.
Left: *Return of the Miners*, 1880 (Rijksmuseum Kröller-Müller, Otterlo).

♦ THE COAL MERCHANT
Van Gogh included this drawing in a letter to Theo in November 1878 (Rijksmuseum Vincent van Gogh, Amsterdam).

LAMPS ♦
Firedamp present in the air in the mines was highly flammable and there was a danger of explosions if it came into contact with heat from candle or torch flames. Miners therefore had special lamps with a shield around the flame.

♦ **WORKING IN THE UNDERGROUND PASSAGES**
To move along the narrowest, sloping passages, the miners had to crawl on all fours in order not to slip. They would kneel or even lie on their backs to work, in conditions that were both dangerous and unhealthy.

♦ **MANUAL LABOUR**
Even though new types of machinery were developed during the nineteenth century to improve productivity in the mines, the main work in the passageways cut in the coal veins was still done manually.

♦ **VENTILATORS FOR FIREDAMP**
Firedamp, a mixture of flammable gases given off by coal, often caused explosions in the mines. It is lighter than air and tends to collect in the upper parts of the mine. Ventilators were introduced to disperse it.

♦ **ON THE SURFACE**
Women and children made up a group of badly-paid, unskilled mine-workers. They were mainly used for tasks on the surface, such as breaking up large pieces of coal.

♦ **COAL CARTS**
Carts filled with coal ran along rails laid in the mine.

♦ **UNDERGROUND**
As soon as they went down into the mine, the colliers were surrounded by darkness, which was broken only by the faint light of oil and benzine lamps.

♦ **IN THE DEPTHS**
When they reached depths of over 200 metres (650 feet), the miners had to work half-naked because of the heat.

A SHOVELLER ♦
After he left the Borinage, van Gogh continued to take an interest in the humblest of labourers. Right: a drawing entitled *The Shoveller's Rest*, 1882 (Private collection).

4. VAN GOGH'S LIFE ♦ *In 1878, wishing to become a lay preacher, van Gogh enrolled in an evangelical training school near Brussels. He failed the course but went on his own initiative to work at Pâturages in the Borinage, a mining region in southern Belgium. The evangelical board relented and took him on for a six-month trial period. Now at Wasmes, he set himself to preach, to help the poor and to look after the sick. He threw himself into his work and wanted to identify with the people in his care. So, to share their experience, he lived in a hovel and slept on the ground. The board disapproved of this extreme way of life and dismissed him in July 1879. He stayed in the Borinage, however, working on his own at Cuesmes for a year. Before he left, he formed a new ambition: to become an artist. In 1880 he settled in Brussels where he made friends with the painter Anton van Rappard. His brother Theo was now sending him a little money.* ⇒

THE POTATO EATERS

♦ **THE LAMP**
A detail from *The Potato Eaters*. The light cast by the lamp creates an intimate family atmosphere among the people seated at the table.

The painting shown below is one of the many pictures of peasant life that van Gogh painted while he stayed with his parents in Nuenen. His father had moved to a new church there in 1883. In this case, he has portrayed a simple family scene. In a humble wooden house, five people seated around a table are having supper. In dim lamplight, some are helping themselves from a plate of boiled potatoes, an old man is drinking and an old woman is pouring coffee.

♦ **FIVE PEASANTS**
Van Gogh returned to the theme of *The Potato Eaters* in 1890, at Saint-Rémy, where he produced the drawing shown above (Rijksmuseum Vincent van Gogh, Amsterdam).

♦ **THE WORK**
The Potato Eaters, 1885, oil on canvas, 81.5 x 114.5 cm (32 x 45 in) (Rijksmuseum Vincent van Gogh, Amsterdam). Van Gogh's signature is legible on the canvas. He painted the picture in April-May 1885, at Nuenen, his father's new parish. It was the final version of a composition he had been working on for several months. At the end of December 1884, he had begun painting portraits of peasants in the area, with a view to producing a picture of a group in an indoor setting. From February 1885, he made drawings and paintings and then a lithograph of a group of people around a dish of potatoes. He described the progress of the composition in his letters to Theo: "I am totally involved in painting heads. I paint during the day, and draw at night. I have painted and drawn in this way at least thirty times ... even at night by lamplight, in the peasants' houses, until it's so dark that I can't see the paint on the palette. This is so that I can understand as much as possible about the effects of light at night, such as, for example, a great dark patch on the wall."

The Potato Eaters *was Vincent van Gogh's first masterpiece and it is very clear that the painting was inspired by his search for an expressive style. His idea was that painting should be more concerned with conveying mood and expressing the inner feeling of the subject, than with representing it in meticulous outward detail. Van Gogh was therefore far removed from the Dutch painting tradition which was based on precise, realistic detail and accurate portrayals. He was much more in tune with the Realist painters of the nineteenth century, who were mostly French but also included some Dutch artists such as Jozef Israëls. Unlike Israëls, however, van Gogh did not treat his subjects with piety, but portrayed their weatherbeaten, work-worn features plainly and honestly.*

♦ **THE LITHOGRAPH**
This is the lithograph that van Gogh made of *The Potato Eaters*, in April 1885 (Rijksmuseum Kröller-Müller, Otterlo).

◆ SIMPLE THINGS
Left and right: details from *The Potato Eaters*. Van Gogh's interest in the poor and his wish to make their everyday life the focus of his artistic efforts link his paintings with the work of novelists such as Emile Zola and Charles Dickens. These two were his favourite authors.

◆ MODELS
At Nuenen, van Gogh used local people as his models and some became his friends. In September 1885, however, rumour had it that he was the father of a child expected by a young peasant girl, Gordina de Groot. The resulting unpopularity of the artist, and his lack of models, were among the reasons why he left Nuenen. Left: *Head of a Peasant Woman*, 1885 (Rijksmuseum Vincent van Gogh, Amsterdam).

◆ THE PEASANT WOMAN
A detail from *The Potato Eaters*, 1885. In a letter to Theo in April 1885, Vincent wrote about the delicate colours that the wind and the sun produced on the peasant women's clothing. The colours he used at this time, however, were rather dark and earthy.

WORK ◆
Van Gogh did not idealize the peasants, but portrayed them as they really were. Right: *Peasant Woman with Spade*, August 1885 (Barber Institute of Fine Arts, Birmingham).

JOZEF ISRAËLS ◆
(1824-1911)
Jozef Israëls was one of the leading members of The Hague School of painting during the second half of the nineteenth century. In contrast to Anton Mauve, he chose to paint urban subjects and family settings. He tended to portray people in a rather sentimental way. Right: Jozef Israëls, *Inside a Hovel*, detail, 1890 (Musée d'Orsay, Paris).

ANTWERP

Belgium gained independence from Holland in 1831 and, in the second half of the nineteenth century, became a prosperous and active nation even though there was rivalry between its Flemish and Walloon communities. The country's economy was built on coalmining, industrial expansion and the resources of its colonies. At the centre of its system of production and trade was the port of Antwerp, a large Flemish city on the Schelde, 90 kilometres (56 miles) from the North Sea. Goods and commodities poured into Antwerp from America, Asia and other parts of the world. Information and ideas from different cultures, including Japan, also flowed in, creating a cosmopolitan atmosphere. However, Antwerp in the nineteenth century did not quite achieve the cultural heights it had reached during the seventeenth century, when it had been home to the great Flemish Baroque painter Peter Paul Rubens.

♦ VAN GOGH AND JAPAN
Many Japanese colour prints were among the more exotic goods arriving in the port of Antwerp. It was when he was in this city that van Gogh first saw examples of them. When he moved to Paris, he had the opportunity to increase his knowledge of Japanese art. He used some Japanese prints in the background of his *Portrait of Père Tanguy* (left), autumn, 1887 (Musée Rodin, Paris).

♦ MANET AND JAPAN
The Impressionist Edouard Manet was one of the first European painters to take an interest in Japanese art. In his *Portrait of Emile Zola* (above), 1868 (Musée d'Orsay, Paris), he included a print by the Japanese artist Kuniaki, in the background on the right; and a Japanese screen on the left.

THE STADHUIS ♦
The Stadhuis (town hall) was on the main square in the centre of Antwerp. Van Gogh made a drawing of it.

THE PORT ♦

Van Gogh moved to Antwerp from rural Nuenen. Living in this lively, cosmopolitan city was some preparation for his next move, to Paris. In Antwerp he produced paintings such as *View of the Port of Antwerp*, 1885 (Rijksmuseum Vincent van Gogh, Amsterdam).

♦ RUBENS

During the three months he spent in Antwerp, van Gogh studied the works of the Flemish master Peter Paul Rubens and developed a great admiration for this artist. In addition, he secured admission to the city's Art Academy, to improve his technical skill as an artist.
Left: Peter Paul Rubens, *Self-portrait with his Wife, Isabella Brant*, 1609-10 (Alte Pinakothek, Munich).

♦ THE SCHELDE

The port of Antwerp grew up on the estuary of the river Schelde, some 90 kilometres (56 miles) from the sea. It was Belgium's largest port and one of the main ports in Europe.

♦ GUILDHALLS

On the main square were the premises of the old guilds, such as those of coopers, haberdashers and wool-makers. Guilds had been powerful in this city where trade was the main occupation.

♦ HIROSHIGE

One of the greatest Japanese artists of the nineteenth century, whose work also came to be appreciated in the West, was Ando Hiroshige (1797-1858).
Left: *The Bridge of Kyoto by the Light of the Moon*, a print by Hiroshige taken from *One Hundred Views of Edo* (1856-59).

5. VAN GOGH'S LIFE ♦ *In 1882 van Gogh was in The Hague, where he painted and developed a relationship with a prostitute known as Sien. For a while he lived with her and thought of marrying her, but eventually he put his artistic career first and they parted in 1883. After spending some time in the province of Drenthe, he moved south to Nuenen in Brabant, where his father now had his parish. During the next two years he produced hundreds of paintings and drawings of the local peasant community. He also read, took piano lessons, and even gave painting lessons to amateur artists. His father died in March 1885 and the local people turned against him. He was falsely accused of fathering the child of a peasant girl whom he had used as a model. In November he moved to Antwerp, where he lodged in a room above an art materials shop. He visited museums to see the works of Rubens. He read Zola, discovered Japanese prints (using them to decorate the walls of his room) and enrolled in the Art Academy. He was never to return to Holland.* ⇒

STILL LIFE

This painting of 1885 shows a seemingly haphazard collection of everyday objects: a straw hat, a meerschaum pipe, a bottle and some containers. As we shall see, however, these are all objects which reappear in a number of van Gogh's paintings, sometimes in connection with a human figure and sometimes not. They were used by van Gogh to study the effects of light and this particular painting probably served as a visual aid in the painting classes he gave while he was in Nuenen.

♦ FAMILIAR OBJECTS
Van Gogh made many drawings of everyday objects in 1885 (Rijksmuseum Vincent van Gogh, Amsterdam).

THE BOTTLE ♦
A detail from *Still Life with Straw Hat*. It was while he was staying in Nuenen that van Gogh began his lengthy research into colour. From then, his paintings were often based on the way colours look under different light conditions.

♦ THE WORK
Still Life with Straw Hat, 1885, oil on canvas, 36 x 53.5 cm (14 x 21 in) (Rijksmuseum Kröller-Müller, Otterlo). The work was painted during the spring-summer of 1885, when van Gogh was still at Nuenen. Although most of his output during this period consisted of portraits of peasants at work and landscape scenes, he also made many studies of birds' nests and other objects.

During the period when he was living in Nuenen (1883-1885), van Gogh decided to begin his own, personal study of light and colour. The letters he wrote to his brother Theo at this time contain meticulous notes on how to create a certain colour and on the reaction of colours to light. He was excited by seeing works by Rembrandt, Rubens and Frans Hals. In a letter written in mid-October 1885, he *considered the use of black: "Can you use black and white, or not? ... Frans Hals uses no fewer than twenty-seven blacks." He concluded: "Black and white have a meaning of their own, and it is a mistake to try to avoid using them." Above all, however, van Gogh was interested in light and the range of colours that he used in his paintings now became markedly brighter.*

♦ THE PIPE
A detail from *Still Life with Straw Hat*. Van Gogh was never separated from his pipe and it often appears in his paintings.

◆ JUST A BRUSH-
STROKE
Left: a detail from
*Still Life with Straw
Hat.* Right: a detail
from *Still Life with
Clogs.*
Both these details
show the same
technique: the effect
of light catching on
an object is conveyed
by brush-strokes in a
paler shade of the
colour used for the
object. The result is
that the object stands
out clearly from the
dark monochrome of
the background.

CLOGS ◆
In the period just
before he left Holland
for good, van Gogh
painted a series of
still lifes. Above: *Still
Life with Clogs*,
(Rijksmuseum
Kröller-Müller,
Otterlo), like *Still Life
with Straw Hat,* was
painted in mid-1885.
Again, in this
painting, van Gogh
was furthering his
study of light and
colour. He wanted to
investigate the
possibilities of dark
colours.

◆ OBJECTS AND
SYMBOLS
Left: *Still Life with
Bible* (Rijksmuseum
Vincent van Gogh,
Amsterdam) was
painted in April 1885.
Van Gogh placed
symbolic meaning on
the everyday objects
in this composition.
The open Bible
represents his father,
who had died the
previous month. The
well-worn copy of
Emile Zola's novel
Joie de Vivre
symbolizes Vincent
himself.

◆ LESSONS FROM THE
MASTERS
Frans Hals, Rubens
and Rembrandt were
among the accepted
Dutch and Flemish
masters whose
paintings van Gogh
most admired. "Frans
Hals," he wrote, "is a
colourist among
colourists ... like
Veronese, Rubens,
Delacroix, Velázquez.
It has been quite
rightly said that Millet,
Rembrandt and, for
example, Israëls are
more harmonizers
than colourists."
Above: Hals, *Banquet
of the Officers of the
Militia Company of
St George*, 1616, detail
(Frans Halsmuseum,
Haarlem).

THEO VAN GOGH

Theo van Gogh was Vincent's favourite brother and, between August 1872 and 27 July 1890, was the main and often the only person to whom Vincent wrote. In his letters, the artist told Theo about his problems and plans and asked for his reactions, which were at times very critical, to his own ideas. Their relationship was close and strong, with Theo not only in the role of confidant but also serving as art expert – he was the manager of an art dealer's – and providing financial help. Theo's profession was one that had arisen from the success of the many art galleries which opened during the second half of the nineteenth century, particularly in Paris.

♦ **THE YOUNGER BROTHER**
Above: a photograph of Theo van Gogh (Rijksmuseum Vincent van Gogh, Amsterdam). Theo was born in Groot Zundert on 1 May 1857 and was the third of six brothers and sisters. He was four years younger than Vincent. In 1889, he married Johanna Bonger. Their son, whom they called Vincent, was born in 1890. Theo died on 25 January 1891, soon after his older brother.

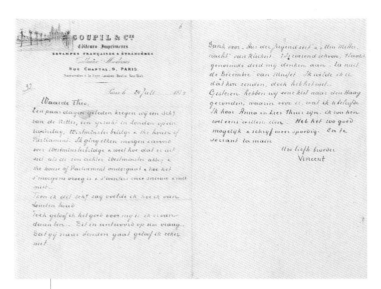

♦ **DEAR THEO**
The letters that Vincent van Gogh wrote have provided information and helped to explain his complex personality, his ideas and his artistic aims and opinions. Of the 821 letters that he wrote, 668 were to Theo. The one reproduced above, written on Goupil's headed notepaper and dated 24 July 1875, was sent from London. Many of the letters also contained rough sketches, portraits, and plans and copies of paintings.

BOUSSOD AND ♦ VALADON
The small gallery managed by Theo was one of many that had opened in Paris in the last decades of the nineteenth century. It was a branch of what had been Goupil's, located at 19 boulevard Montmartre. By Theo's time it was Boussod and Valadon.

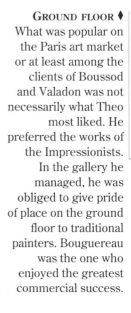

GROUND FLOOR ♦
What was popular on the Paris art market or at least among the clients of Boussod and Valadon was not necessarily what Theo most liked. He preferred the works of the Impressionists. In the gallery he managed, he was obliged to give pride of place on the ground floor to traditional painters. Bouguereau was the one who enjoyed the greatest commercial success.

6. VAN GOGH'S LIFE ♦ *Van Gogh took courses at the Art Academy in Antwerp, even studying at night, but despite these efforts he was still considered "unsuitable" to proceed to the next level of tuition. He had argued with some of the conventional teaching. He did not wait for official notification of his examination results and left for Paris. He arrived there unexpectedly on 28 February 1886 and sent a note to his brother Theo, who met him at the Louvre. At that time, Theo was busily involved in running the Boussod and Valadon gallery and he would really have preferred Vincent to return home to their mother in Brabant. He tried to persuade him to do so, but Vincent remained obstinate that he would stay. Theo continued to be his one true support, both financially and morally.* ⟫

♦ **MEZZANINE**
Theo used the mezzanine of his gallery to show paintings by Corot, Daumier, Manet, Renoir, Monet and, in particular, Degas to his more sophisticated clients.

♦ **THE ART DEALER**
Theo van Gogh stayed with the art-dealing company, Goupil's, all his working life. He spent time in the branches in Brussels and The Hague (above) and finally moved to Paris. He had a very open mind when considering the work of contemporary artists and was one of the first people to appreciate the value of his brother Vincent's work. He tried, with little success, to sell it.

Paris in 1886

When Vincent van Gogh arrived in Paris in 1886, the art world was beginning to recognize the importance of the controversial new paintings that had appeared in previous years. The Impressionists were holding their eighth and last exhibition, but some of the movement's best-known members, including Renoir and Monet, had refused to show their work. Two newcomers, Seurat and Signac, along with Pissarro, showed pictures at the exhibition in a new style now often known as "Neo-Impressionist". Other names for it, based on the technique employed, were "divisionist" and "pointillist". The variety of artistic styles was gradually increasing, with new figures on the scene such as Odilon Redon, Paul Gauguin, the Italian Giovanni Boldini and the eccentric Henri Rousseau, nicknamed "le Douanier Rousseau" because he worked for the Paris customs office.

♦ **THE CORMON ATELIER**
One of the most prestigious places to study in Paris was the studio of Fernand Cormon. He was a very successful, though conventional painter and a good teacher. In his studio (shown above in a photograph of 1886) van Gogh met Bernard, Anquetin and Toulouse-Lautrec.

7. VAN GOGH'S LIFE ♦ *Vincent shared Theo's apartment in the rue Laval (now rue Victor-Massé), not too far from the gallery that his brother managed. In June 1886, they moved to a larger apartment in the rue Lepic. Vincent was determined to make the most of Paris. He painted furiously, met many fellow artists and studied at the Cormon atelier, one of the city's best-known teaching studios. Theo put up with his brother's unpredictable mood-swings and wrote: "It's as if he were two completely different people. One is sweet, sensitive and extraordinarily gifted; the other egotistical and hard-hearted." Meanwhile their mother moved away from Nuenen and many of Vincent's works, left behind there, were lost as a result.* ⇉→

THE IMPRESSIONISTS ♦ 1
By 1886 the Impressionists were winning their battle and the value of their work had begun to be recognized.

1. Claude Monet, *Woman with Parasol*, detail, 1886 (Musée d'Orsay, Paris); 2. Edgar Degas, *The Tub*, 1886 (Musée d'Orsay, Paris); 3. Pierre-Auguste Renoir, *The Great Bathers*, 1884-87 (Museum of Art, Philadelphia).

THE DIVISIONISTS ♦ 1
The most innovative works at the 1886 Impressionist exhibition were those of the divisionist painters, who are also called pointillists or Neo-Impressionists. Seurat's *La Grande Jatte* caused a sensation.

1. Camille Pissarro, *The Gleaners*, detail, 1889 (Öffentliche Kunstsammlung, Basel); 2. Georges Seurat, *La Grande Jatte*, 1884-86 (Art Institute, Chicago); 3. Paul Signac, *The Dining Room*, detail, 1886-87 (Rijksmuseum Kröller-Müller, Otterlo).

NEW ARTISTS ♦ 1
Henri Rousseau (1844-1910), known as Le Douanier, and the Italian Giovanni Boldini (1842-1931) were among the new artists to emerge in Paris in the 1880s and 1890s.

1. Giovanni Boldini, *Portrait of Giuseppe Verdi*, 1886 (Galleria Nazionale di Arte Moderna, Rome); 2. Henri Rousseau, *Carnival Night*, detail, 1886 (Museum of Art, Philadelphia); 3. Henri Rousseau, *A Riverbank*, 1886 (Private collection, Paris).

THE EIFFEL TOWER

From 1851 onwards, exhibitions of manufactures and crafts from around the world were held periodically in the capital cities of Europe and America. People visiting the huge International Exhibitions, or World Fairs, held in London, New York and Paris could see the material results of the faith that had been placed in science and view the latest developments in technology. When van Gogh arrived in Paris in 1886, the city was already preparing for the International Exhibition that was to be held there in 1889, to celebrate the centenary of the French Revolution. The Eiffel Tower was built as a gateway to the Exhibition; it became a permanent symbol of the French capital.

♦ **EIFFEL, THE ENGINEER** (1832-1923) Alexandre-Gustave Eiffel was a great engineer and entrepreneur. A specialist in building work using iron and steel, he had also designed the steel framework for the Statue of Liberty in New York Harbour. Left: a portrait by Viesseux (Musée d'Orsay, Paris).

A WONDER ♦ OF TECHNOLOGY The pieces of iron from which the tower was built were prepared in a machine shop, with great accuracy, and then put together, on site, by small teams of specialist workers.

♦**THE FINISHED TOWER** The tower weighs about 9,500,000 kilograms (9,350 tons). Its four uprights merge and rise to a height of 300 metres (984 feet) and it has three platforms, with restaurants and offices. The tower was ready for the opening of the International Exhibition on 31 March 1889, though the third platform was not added until May.

♦**A PUBLIC SUCCESS** The International Exhibition lasted 173 days, during which time 1,900,000 people visited the Eiffel Tower. Four staircases, with a total of 1,792 steps, led to the uppermost platform. Eiffel had a lavishly decorated office at the top of the tower which he also used as a laboratory for studying aerodynamics, astronomy and meteorology.

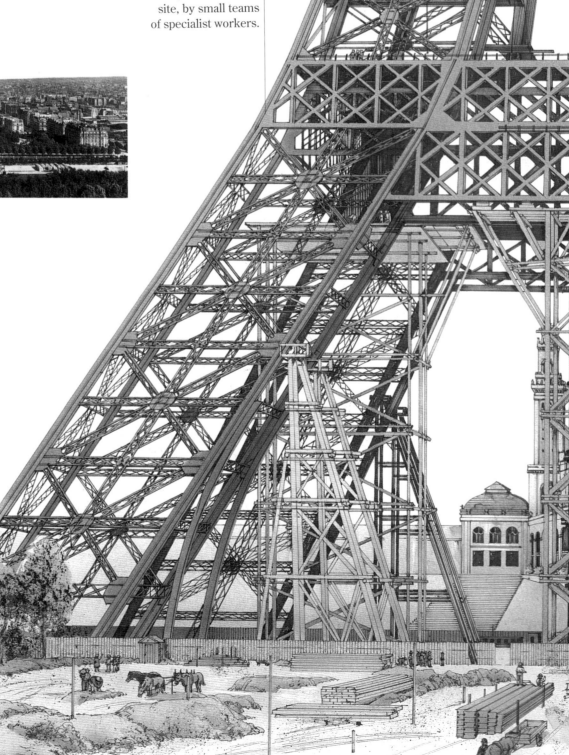

PAINTINGS OF THE ◆ TOWER
Some sections of intellectual society were critical of the tower, but there were many artists who did not share this view. They were happy to include the tower in their paintings of the city.
Right: a detail from Henri Rousseau's *Self-portrait – Landscape*, 1889-90 (Národni Galerie, Prague).

POSTERS OF THE ◆ TOWER
Many posters were printed to mark the opening of the Eiffel Tower in 1889. The International Exhibition was a spectacular and cosmopolitan event, and its success helped France's recovery after the country's traumatic defeat by Prussia nineteen years earlier.

◆ THE UPRIGHTS
The tower is supported by four uprights and each of these has its own lift which ascends on a curve. Two of the lifts go to the first platform and two to the second. A fifth lift travels the 78 metres (256 feet) between the second and third levels.

◆ PRAISE AND CRITICISM
After the tower had been built, Gustave Eiffel was decorated with France's highest award, the Legion of Honour, while a large number of writers, artists and musicians "protested with all their strength and with all their indignation, in the name of French taste which had been disregarded" against the building of the "useless and monstrous Eiffel Tower" in the heart of the city. In response to these criticisms, Eiffel wrote an article claiming that the tower had an abstract beauty of its own. It was, he said, the product of logic and science and its very existence was a "symbol of man's victory over the problems imposed by the laws of nature".

◆ WOODEN SUPPORTS
Building such a tall metal structure was an extraordinary undertaking. Huge wooden supports were needed when work began. Once the first platform had been completed, the wooden structures were dismantled.

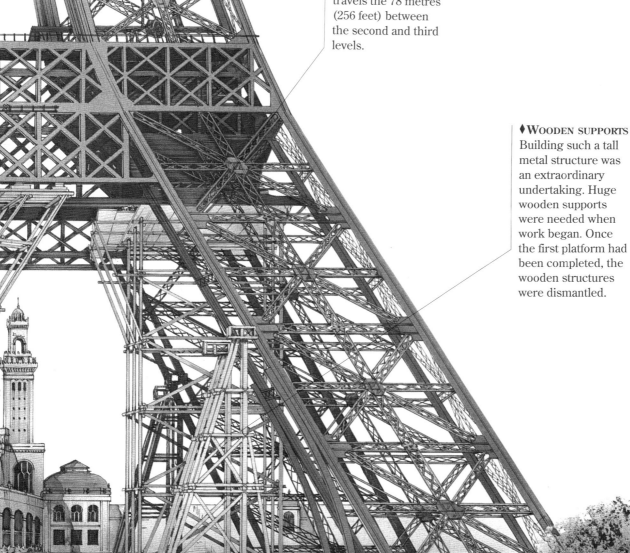

ASNIÈRES

The small Parisian suburb of Asnières, with its bridges over the Seine, fishing boats moored along the riverbanks, tree-lined avenues and cafés, had already been the setting of many Impressionist paintings. Monet, Pissarro, Renoir and Caillebotte had all found that Asnières had the right atmosphere for painting "en plein air" (in the open). Van Gogh followed in their footsteps. In the painting shown here, he captured one of the best-known views of Asnières: a spot where the river was crossed by a series of arched bridges. One of the bridges was for the railway.

♦ **THE WORK**
Bridges at Asnières, 1887, oil on canvas, 52 x 65 cm (20½ x 25½ in) (Bührle Collection, Zurich). Van Gogh painted this work during the summer of 1887 in Asnières, a suburb of Paris that he had discovered thanks to Emile Bernard (1868-1941).
Bernard was an intelligent and highly talented young artist and friend of Paul Gauguin, and he and van Gogh had met in 1886 in Fernand Cormon's studio, where they were both studying painting.
During his stay in Paris, Vincent often accompanied Bernard to Asnières, to paint "en plein air" as the Impressionists had done. Over a period of two years, van Gogh painted many versions of the bridges that cross the river there.

♦ **BERNARD'S VIEW OF ASNIÈRES**
Emile Bernard also painted *Bridges at* *Asnières* (Museum of Modern Art, New York) during the summer of 1887.

♦ **SOLITARY FIGURES**
Above and below: details from *Bridges at Asnières*.

"While painting at Asnières, I saw more colours than I have ever seen before." Behind these words of van Gogh is the sense that he was trying to get close to Impressionism. He studied the same techniques, chose the same subjects and went to the same places as the Impressionists had done.

He painted constantly, to try to acquire the ability they had to convey the quality of the atmosphere and light by the use of colour. He changed from his original tendency towards Realism and was attracted instead by the idea of capturing fleeting impressions by working rapidly on the spot.

♦ **WITH BERNARD IN ASNIÈRES**
Bernard and van Gogh (with his back turned) talking by the Seine in 1886.

♦ **IMPRESSIONIST SUBJECTS AND TECHNIQUES**
Above and below: details from *Bridges at Asnières* show van Gogh's use of pure colours applied with rapid and short brush-strokes. The effect achieved by this technique is dynamic. The train introduces a modern theme into the natural surroundings.

A PERIOD OF STUDY ♦
The two years from 1886 to 1888 in Paris were a period of study for van Gogh. Thanks to his brother's contacts, he was also able to meet many of the most important contemporary artists. Vincent painted constantly and, although he showed a distinct preference for landscape painting – and for countryside rather than urban scenes – he did not neglect to practise in other fields of art, such as still life and portrait-painting. The greatest changes in his work at this time can be seen mainly in the views and still lifes that he produced: he now used lighter colours.

Above right: *Still Life with Lemons*, 1887 (Rijksmuseum Vincent van Gogh, Amsterdam).
Right: *Portrait of the Art Dealer Alexander Reid*, 1887 (Art Gallery and Museum, Glasgow).

THE DIVISIONISTS

At the eighth Impressionist exhibition in Paris in 1886, the most innovative works were those of the divisionists. Seurat's *La Grande Jatte* caused a sensation. Instead of mixing colours on his palette, the artist had applied small dots of pure colours to the canvas, so that, seen from a distance, these colours blended (optical mixing). The French critic Félix Fénéon coined the word "pointillism" to describe this painting technique and called the artists who used it "Neo-Impressionists", but Seurat preferred the term "divisionism". The divisionists had carried further the Impressionists' study of light effects. Pissarro said that the "romantic" and "scientific" Impressionists had now parted company.

♦ SEURAT AND CHEVREUL'S WHEEL
Georges Seurat took an interest in scientific works and Eugène Chevreul's studies, published in 1839, had a fundamental influence on his own artistic development. In particular, Seurat used Chevreul's colour wheel, which provided vital clues to the use of complementary colours, for example demonstrating that every colour tends to introduce a tint of its complementary colour into weaker colours next to it.

♦ GEORGES SEURAT (1859-1891)
Coming from an upper middle-class family in Paris, Seurat was able to set up his own studio in 1872.
He studied the painting of Piero della Francesca, and the work of other classical artists, with great enthusiasm, and also took a keen interest in reading scientific treatises.
He worked tirelessly on his great compositions. First he made notes from life, including studies of colours recorded in black and white, and then he spent a great deal of time in his studio, painting. He was a strong personality who attracted a considerable following, even at his young age.
A sudden illness ended his short life on 29 March 1891, and so his last masterpiece, *The Circus*, was left unfinished.

8. VAN GOGH'S LIFE ♦ *Van Gogh attended the studio of Fernand Cormon, hoping that the master would help him to improve his technique. In fact, the main benefit of working there proved to be that he met a number of young artists such as Emile Bernard, Henri de Toulouse-Lautrec and Louis Anquetin. He made other contacts through his brother Theo. Despite the Boussod and Valadon directors, who disapproved of unconventional works, Theo set himself to promote Impressionist painting and other new trends in art. He introduced Vincent to the great Impressionist figures, Monet, Pissarro, Sisley and Renoir, and to younger innovators such as Signac and Seurat.* ⇒♦

♦ THE CIRCUS PARADE
Above and left: details from Georges Seurat's *The Circus Parade*, 1887-88 (Metropolitan Museum, New York). Seurat was the artist who used the divisionist style most rigorously. In this painting, the coloured dots are arranged in such a way that they create a halo effect around the figures.

P. Signac .88
Dp.182

♦ **PAUL SIGNAC**
(1863-1935)
From 1891, Paul Signac replaced his friend Seurat as leader of the Neo-Impressionist group. He came from a well-to-do family and was a frequent visitor to fashionable beach resorts in the south of France. From the time he met Seurat in 1884, he consistently adopted the divisionist technique.

Left: *The Lighthouse at Portrieux*, 1888 (Private collection); and below: a detail from the painting.

♦ **DOTS OF COLOUR**
Divisionism, or pointillism, is a painting technique in which regular dots of pure colour are applied with small brush-strokes. The term "divisionism" came from the fact that different colours of paint were kept separate or "divided". Most nineteenth-century painters mixed their colours on the palette. The Impressionists used various dabs, strokes or dots of pure colour, but in spontaneous, unplanned fashion. Then Seurat produced the "scientific" version known as divisionism.
The works reproduced here help to explain the technique. Dots of pure colours were applied separately to the canvas, but when the picture is viewed from a distance, those colours combine on the retina of the viewer's eye. The effect is that the painting looks bright and luminous. Another divisionist feature is a kind of dotted frame around the picture. This serves to blend the colours of the painting with the colour of the mount or frame chosen for it. Divisionist ideas were based on the findings of nineteenth-century scientists studying optics. One of these was the Frenchman Eugène Chevreul (1786-1889), photographed (above) on his one hundredth birthday by the famous Nadar.

MAXIMILIEN LUCE ♦
Right: *Paris from Montmartre*, 1887 (Musée du Petit Palais, Geneva) by the Parisian Maximilien Luce (1858-1941); and above: a detail of the painting.
Luce became a divisionist after Seurat's success in 1886-87. However, his interpretation of the divisionist method was less strict than Seurat's. His dots are distributed more freely and the colours less "scientifically" juxtaposed. Luce was deeply committed to contemporary social protest movements and most of his paintings concentrate on the life of the working classes. The painting shown here is an exception.

BOULEVARD DE CLICHY

Van Gogh preferred the countryside to the city. He did not even like Paris, one of the favourite subjects of painters such as Pissarro, Degas and Monet. Nonetheless, in his desire to master Impressionist and Neo-Impressionist techniques, he often devoted himself to portraying urban scenes such as this: a corner of a boulevard with a few cold passers-by enveloped in a grey light.

♦ **DETAILS OF THE BOULEVARD**
Above and below: details from *Boulevard de Clichy*.

♦ **THE WORK**
Boulevard de Clichy, 1887, oil on canvas, 46.5 x 55 cm (18 x 21 in) (Rijksmuseum Vincent van Gogh, Amsterdam). The painting dates from February-March 1887. Van Gogh preferred the spaciousness of the Seine at Asnières, and the light and air of the open countryside, to built-up city surroundings. However, he did not neglect to paint urban subjects. The boulevard de Clichy lay at the foot of hilly Montmartre, not far from the apartment that he shared with his brother Theo. To produce works like this one, Vincent usually sketched the scene on site, making notes about the colours he would use when painting the final version.

♦ **THE OTHER FACE OF MONTMARTRE**
In *Vegetable Gardens in Montmartre*, 1887 (Stedelijk Museum, Amsterdam), van Gogh showed the area's rural side.

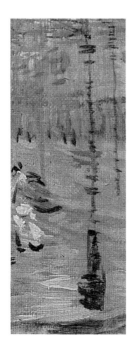

Cityscapes – images of modern daily life – were one of the favourite subjects of the Impressionist painters. Van Gogh also took up the challenge of painting the city, including the lively district of Montmartre, full of cafés and inhabited by artists. However, he preferred its more rural areas, where the city ended and vegetable gardens began. It is evident from some works from this period that van Gogh was trying to master the techniques of the divisionists, using pure, unmixed colours and small brush-strokes. But he was too much an individualist to accept the divisionist discipline and adapted the method to his own type of expression.

♦ **A STUDY**
A preparatory drawing for *Boulevard de Clichy*, early 1887 (Rijksmuseum Vincent van Gog, Amsterdam)

♦A PERIOD OF STUDY
These details from *Boulevard de Clichy* show that, by early 1887, van Gogh had already learned a great deal from his time in Paris. A few brush-strokes create the impression of a human figure (left) or a tree (right). The colours are pure and much lighter than the earthy tones of his early works.

♦ASNIÈRES AGAIN
With the onset of better weather, van Gogh left the city to paint "en plein air" in the countryside. *Restaurant "La Sirène"* (Musée d'Orsay, Paris) was painted in Asnières during the summer of 1887, and shows how far van Gogh's use of Impressionist techniques had advanced.

♦VASES OF FLOWERS
This detail from *Interior of a Restaurant* shows how van Gogh interpreted divisionism: he combined different types of brush-stroke with the dots of colour, producing a less meticulous but more vital result.

FOLLOWING SEURAT ♦
Interior of a Restaurant, summer 1887 (Rijksmuseum Kröller-Müller, Otterlo), was as close as van Gogh came to the divisionism of Seurat and Signac. Using this technique took time, for it required meticulous work. Van Gogh, on the other hand, wanted to express himself quickly.

THE BELLE EPOQUE

The Belle Epoque was the leisured age enjoyed by the well-to-do at the end of the nineteenth century, especially in sophisticated cites such as Paris. The atmosphere of Parisian theatres, nightclubs and cafés was captured by artists such as Toulouse-Lautrec. In a café-concert, or café-chantant, music was played as drinks and meals were served. Cabarets began as taverns where artists met, but later became venues for poetry readings, music and avant-garde theatre. An off-shoot of the café-chantant and music hall was the "variety", a theatre for musical comedy and sketches. The circus became fashionable too.

♦ WINDMILLS
There were still a few windmills ("moulins" in French) in Montmartre at the end of the nineteenth century. They must have reminded van Gogh of his native country.
Left: van Gogh, *Moulin de Blute-fin*, summer 1886 (Art Gallery and Museum, Glasgow).

♦ THE MOULIN DE LA GALETTE
Having ceased to be a flour mill, the Moulin de la Galette (seen here in a photograph of the time) became one of the most popular and famous dance halls in Montmartre during the nineteenth century. It was named after the pancakes ("galettes" in French) that were served there. A new use was found for the old mill sails: they became advertising signs for the dance hall.

♦ AGOSTINA SEGATORI
One of the cafés that van Gogh visited was the Tambourin, run by Agostina Segatori. A former model of Corot, she was close to the group of artists with whom van Gogh was friendly.
Left: Vincent van Gogh, *Portrait of Agostina Segatori at the Tambourin*, 1887 (Rijksmuseum Vincent van Gogh, Amsterdam).

9. VAN GOGH'S LIFE ♦ *Van Gogh continued to see his friends Bernard and Signac in 1887 and also had a love affair with Agostina Segatori, an Italian model who had posed for Corot. She owned the Tambourin, a café on boulevard de Clichy, where Vincent put on an exhibition of Japanese prints. He became friendly with Père Tanguy, who sold paints and other artists' materials. In his shop on the rue Clauzel, it was always possible to meet other artists, exhibit paintings and get some hot food. But eventually van Gogh grew tired of Paris, writing to Theo: "I want to escape to some place in the south where there aren't so many painters who disgust me as men."* ⇒+

♦ ENTERTAINMENT
A range of entertainment was provided at the Moulin Rouge. It was a café-concert, theatre and music hall. It was luxuriously decorated, and had small tables, a dance floor and gardens.

DANCERS ♦
The shows at the Moulin Rouge were famous and the greatest stars of dancing performed there. Fashionable dances were the can-can, the quadrille and the chahut.

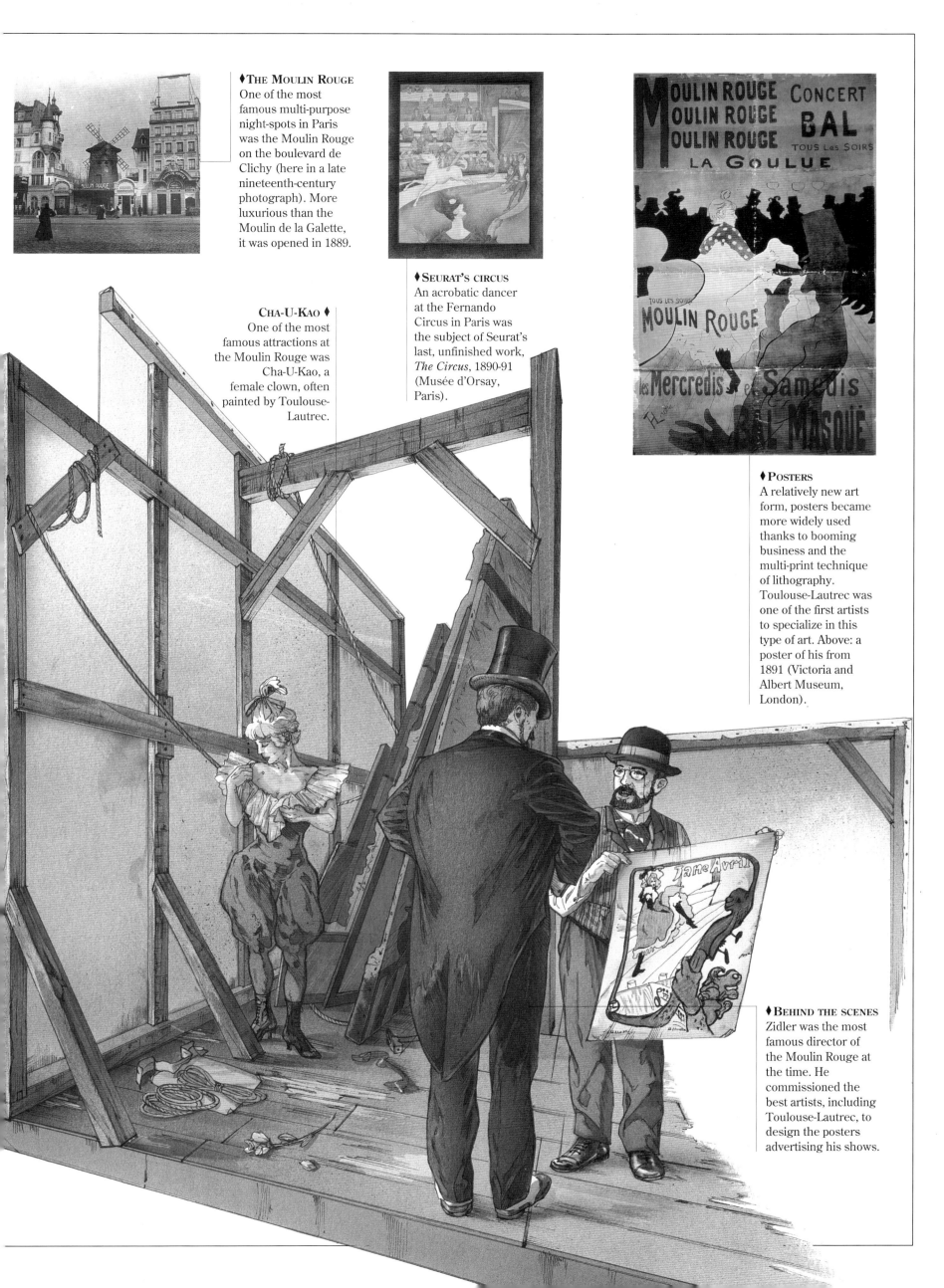

♦ THE MOULIN ROUGE
One of the most famous multi-purpose night-spots in Paris was the Moulin Rouge on the boulevard de Clichy (here in a late nineteenth-century photograph). More luxurious than the Moulin de la Galette, it was opened in 1889.

CHA-U-KAO ♦
One of the most famous attractions at the Moulin Rouge was Cha-U-Kao, a female clown, often painted by Toulouse-Lautrec.

♦ SEURAT'S CIRCUS
An acrobatic dancer at the Fernando Circus in Paris was the subject of Seurat's last, unfinished work, *The Circus*, 1890-91 (Musée d'Orsay, Paris).

♦ POSTERS
A relatively new art form, posters became more widely used thanks to booming business and the multi-print technique of lithography. Toulouse-Lautrec was one of the first artists to specialize in this type of art. Above: a poster of his from 1891 (Victoria and Albert Museum, London).

♦ BEHIND THE SCENES
Zidler was the most famous director of the Moulin Rouge at the time. He commissioned the best artists, including Toulouse-Lautrec, to design the posters advertising his shows.

ARTISTS OF THE PETIT BOULEVARD

While in Paris van Gogh did not mix with the most famous Impressionists, whom he called "of the Grand Boulevard". Rather, he painted, talked and exhibited his work with a smaller group of young artists whom he described as "of the Petit Boulevard" – Bernard, Toulouse-Lautrec and Anquetin. Meanwhile, there were many disputes in the Paris art world, particularly between Bernard and the group led by Seurat and Signac, who were accused of being excessively technical, scientific and cold. Van Gogh wanted to form a harmonious and unified community of artists, modelled on medieval brotherhoods and close to the people. He tried to organize exhibitions in his local cafés and bistros, to suit the tastes of ordinary men and women. There was a short happy period of sharing ideas, but soon all the members of the group went their separate ways.

♦ **AN EXHIBITION AT THE TAMBOURIN**
The young artists of the "Petit Boulevard" were able to exhibit their works when their friends kindly offered their cafés or restaurants as venues. Agostina Segatori allowed van Gogh to exhibit Japanese prints at her café, the Tambourin, during the spring of 1887. She was probably the model for his painting of *The Italian Woman* (left), December 1887 (Musée d'Orsay, Paris).

♦ **HENRI DE TOULOUSE-LAUTREC**
Henri de Toulouse-Lautrec (1864-1901) was left with stunted legs after two falls during his teens. Later, he became the archetypal isolated and rebellious artist and is best known for his clear-eyed pictures of Paris nightlife, including the dancers at the Moulin Rouge; but he had not yet gained this reputation when he was part of the "Petit Boulevard" group and friendly with van Gogh. Two of his works from this period are reproduced here. Far left: *Carmen*, 1884 (Sterling and Francine Clark Art Institute, Williamstown, Massachusetts). Left: *Portrait of the Countess de Toulouse-Lautrec in the salon of the château at Malromé*, 1886-87 (Musée Lautrec, Albi).

10. VAN GOGH'S LIFE ♦ *Young artists in Montmartre would meet at Père Tanguy's, look at paintings and discuss ideas heatedly. It was here that van Gogh often saw Paul Gauguin. But he could not stand all the disputes and would often leave without having said a word. He wrote to Bernard: "If we really believe that Signac and the other 'pointillists' often do good work, then instead of tearing their paintings to pieces we should give them recognition and talk about them respectfully. Otherwise we become narrow-minded sectarians." At the same time, it was in his own nature to create difficult situations. Theo wrote to their sister that life with Vincent was "intolerable", but eventually matters improved. Van Gogh organized some small exhibitions of the "Petit Boulevard" in some of the Montmartre cafés.* ≫✦

♦ **LOUIS ANQUETIN**
Louis Anquetin (1861-1932) was another member of the "Petit Boulevard" group. He pioneered cloisonnism with Bernard, to whom he dedicated his *Portrait of Emile Bernard*, c.1887 (Rijksmuseum Vincent van Gogh, Amsterdam).

♦ **EMILE BERNARD**
Emile Bernard (1868-1941) was one of the brightest intellects in the Paris art world. He turned away from Impressionism and divisionism, using symbolism and creating an atmosphere of mystery in which people and things took on a spiritual meaning. He also adopted a new technique, cloisonnism, in which areas of bright, flat colour were enclosed by dark outlines. Far left: clearly outlined, simplified forms and intense colours, in a detail from *Breton Women in the Fields*, 1888 (Private collection). Left: *Self-portrait, to my Friend Vincent*, 1888 (Rijksmuseum Vincent van Gogh, Amsterdam).

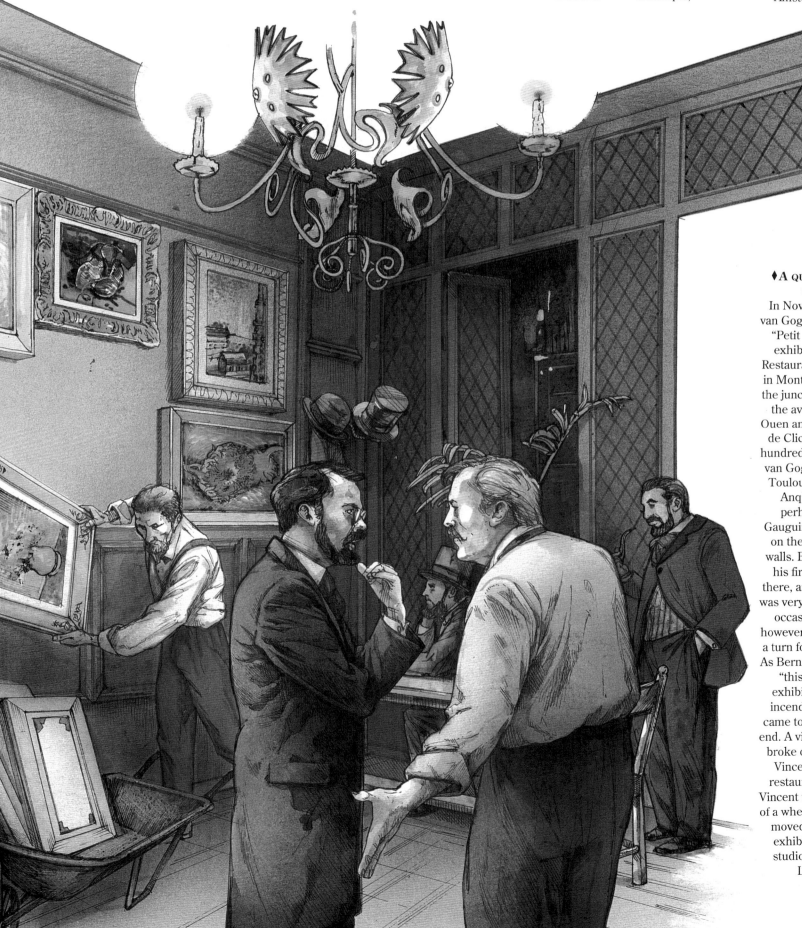

♦ **A QUARREL AT A SHOW**
In November 1887 van Gogh organized a "Petit Boulevard" exhibition at the Restaurant du Chalet in Montmartre, near the junction between the avenue Saint-Ouen and the avenue de Clichy. About a hundred paintings by van Gogh, Bernard, Toulouse-Lautrec, Anquetin and perhaps even Gauguin were hung on the restaurant walls. Bernard sold his first painting there, and van Gogh was very proud of the occasion. Later, however, things took a turn for the worse. As Bernard reported, "this left-wing exhibition of our incendiary works came to a miserable end. A violent quarrel broke out between Vincent and the restaurant owner. Vincent then got hold of a wheelbarrow and moved the whole exhibition to his studio in the rue Lepic."

SELF-PORTRAIT IN FRONT OF THE EASEL

This work was painted at a critical time in van Gogh's life and in his development as an artist, at the end of his stay in Paris. In the grip of depression, he looked for answers to many questions about himself. Painting a self-portrait was a way of delving deep into his own personality.

♦ **THE LOOK**
More than showing how van Gogh's appearance altered over time, his self-portraits are evidence of his volatile character. He was given to outbursts of anger, yet capable of great tenderness. Above: *Self-portrait*, 1887 (Rijksmuseum Kröller-Müller, Otterlo).

♦ **THE WORK**
Self-portrait in front of the Easel, 1888, oil on canvas, 65.5 x 50.5 cm (26 x 20 in) (Rijksmuseum Vincent van Gogh, Amsterdam). Dated January 1888, this was one of the last works van Gogh painted in Paris. At this time he was going through a period of deep depression. Painting did not always help him overcome the attacks, but more and more often, during his last months in the city, he would shut himself in his studio and examine his face in the mirror, to produce a self-portrait. He painted about ten in this way and explained in a letter to his sister Wilhelmina: "My intention is to show that a variety of very different portraits can be made of the same person." The letter also contains information about the colours he used: "A basic palette of lemon yellow, vermilion, malachite green and cobalt blue. Just all the basic palette colours, except the orange for the beard. The figure is set against a grey-blue background."

Because it was difficult and, at times, impossible to find models, van Gogh often used himself as the subject for his paintings. The self-portraits he produced were not as many in number as those painted by his fellow Dutch artist Rembrandt, but nonetheless they provide much evidence of his appearance and, above all, of his moods. There are forty-three moving and sometimes dramatic pictures of van Gogh, in all of which the eyes – often looking in two different directions – seem to be trying to make contact and communicate with the viewer.

♦ **A DRAWING**
Detail from a *Self-portrait*, 1887 (Rijksmuseum Vincent van Gogh, Amsterdam).

♦ **THE DARK HAT**
This dark-toned *Self-portrait* dates from 1886 or may even belong to the Nuenen period (Rijksmuseum Vincent van Gogh, Amsterdam).

♦ **TWO YEARS EARLIER**
Van Gogh painted this *Self-portrait in front of the Easel* in 1886 (Rijksmuseum Vincent van Gogh, Amsterdam). The dark colours are a sign that it belongs to the period van Gogh spent in Nuenen or Antwerp or to his early months in Paris.

◆ **THE LIGHT HAT**
Self-portrait with Felt Hat, 1887-88 (Rijksmuseum Vincent van Gogh, Amsterdam). Now the colours are lighter and applied with Impressionist brush-strokes.

THE STRAW HAT ◆
Van Gogh looked unkempt and dressed carelessly. He loved hats and pipes, and both appear in this *Self-portrait*, painted in Arles in 1888 (Rijksmuseum Vincent van Gogh, Amsterdam).

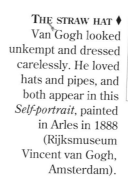

LOST IN THOUGHT ◆
This *Self-portrait* (Musée d'Orsay, Paris) was painted in 1889 in the asylum at Saint-Rémy. Van Gogh looks "as pale as the devil", as he himself wrote to Theo.

◆ **LIKENESS**
A detail from *Self-portrait in front of the Easel*. Van Gogh wrote to his sister: "It is not easy to paint a self-portrait, at least when it has to be different from a photograph"; the aim was "to achieve a deeper resemblance than in a photograph".

◆ **TOOLS OF THE TRADE**
A detail from *Self-portrait in front of the Easel*. The brushes and palette are smeared with the pure colours van Gogh used in his painting: vermilion, blue, yellow and green.

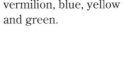

HOW OTHERS ◆
PORTRAYED VAN GOGH
Many of van Gogh's friends, including Lautrec, Bernard and Gauguin, painted portraits of him. This one is by John Russell, 1886 (Rijksmuseum Vincent van Gogh, Amsterdam).

PAINTERS IN PROVENCE

The colours, atmosphere and scenery of Provence had attracted artists long before van Gogh. Several of the Impressionists spent some time in the South of France, notably Monet and Renoir, who eventually made his home there. Cézanne and Monticelli were Southerners who spent only a limited time in Paris before returning to their roots. One thing all the artists who came to Provence had in common was the importance that they placed on the study of colour.

Mediterranean Sea

♦ AN ANCIENT REGION
Provence is a large, mountainous region in southern France. Its largest city is Marseille. To the east are the Alps, to the west, the river Rhône and to the south, the Mediterranean. It was an ancient Roman province. In the Middle Ages, the troubadours of Provence composed superb poetry and music.

VAN GOGH'S ♦ PROVENCE
In a letter to his sister, van Gogh explained: "Today my palette is filled with colours: sky blue, pink, orange, vermilion."
Right: *Harvest on the Plain of La Crau*, 1888 (Rijksmuseum Vincent van Gogh, Amsterdam).

FRUIT TREES ♦
Fruit trees were one of the first subjects that van Gogh painted in Arles. The influence of Japanese art shows in *Pink Peach Tree in Blossom (Souvenir de Mauve)*, 1888 (Rijksmuseum Kröller-Müller, Otterlo).

♦ THE LANGLOIS BRIDGE
Below: *The Langlois Bridge with Women Washing*, March 1888 (Rijksmuseum Kröller-Müller, Otterlo).
Van Gogh drew and painted many versions of the view of this bridge, which he discovered on his expeditions into the countryside around Arles. Aspects of this painting are reminiscent of Japanese prints of bridges.

♦ **BRAQUE**
With Pablo Picasso, Georges Braque (1882-1963) developed Cubism. He spent a short time in Provence in 1906-1907, attracted by the colours of the area and by its links with Cézanne, who was revered by many painters of Braque's generation.
Left: Braque, *Landscape at La Ciotat*, 1906 (Galerie Beyeler, Basel).

♦ **SIGNAC**
The divisionist painter Paul Signac (1863-1935) was one of the most regular visitors to the South of France. A friend of Seurat and van Gogh, he lived in Saint-Tropez for about twenty years.
Left: Signac, *Saint-Tropez – Storm*, 1895 (Musée de l'Annonciade, Saint-Tropez).

♦ **CÉZANNE**
Paul Cézanne (1839-1906) was born and died in Aix-en-Provence. He became an Impressionist for a time, but eventually created his own unique style, having a powerful influence on the development of modern art.
Above: Cézanne, *Mont Sainte-Victoire*, c.1887 (Courtauld Institute Galleries, London).

♦ **GUIGOU**
There had been an active school of local painters in Provence since the middle of the nineteenth century. Paul Guigou (1834-1871) painted *The Hills of Allauch near Marseille*, 1863 (Musée des Beaux-Arts, Marseille), in a straightforward Realist style.

♦ **MATISSE**
One of the greatest artists of modern times, Henri Matisse (1869-1954) was first struck by the colours of the South on the island of Corsica. He then spent several summers in Provence and later moved permanently to Nice.
Left: Matisse, *Collioure*, 1905 (Musée de l'Annonciade, Saint-Tropez).

11. VAN GOGH'S LIFE ♦ *In 1888, Vincent left Paris and went to live in Arles, in Provence. From there he wrote to his brother Theo: "I can hardly imagine coming back to work in Paris, unless there was a little place there to escape to, where one could recover and regain a sense of calm and some self-esteem. Without that, one would inevitably go mad." He set to work immediately in Arles and regularly sent his canvases to Theo, who was supporting him by sending him 250 francs a month. On 1 May, he rented a wing of a building called the Yellow House with the intention of starting an artists' colony like the one at Pont-Aven in Brittany where his friend Paul Gauguin was staying.* ➤

VAN GOGH'S TECHNIQUE

As he studied painting, van Gogh experimented with all the styles and techniques of his time. His first models were Realist works in the style of Millet and the dark-coloured paintings of his native Holland. Then he practised using the brighter colours of the Impressionists, trying to discover how to capture on the canvas the light and atmosphere of a particular moment. Studying divisionism represented an attempt to adopt a more scientific approach to his painting. Finally, he absorbed all of these influences, using whichever approach seemed suitable and developing a style of his own, characterized by strength and speedy execution. He was always ready to try new ideas, from squeezing paint directly out of the tube on to the canvas to painting night scenes, working in the open air by candlelight.

♦ REFLECTIONS
Vincent van Gogh, *Starry Night on the Rhône*, 1888 (Musée d'Orsay, Paris).

♦ SUNFLOWERS
In 1888, Paul Gauguin painted this *Portrait of Van Gogh Painting Sunflowers* (Rijksmuseum Vincent van Gogh, Amsterdam). Vincent said: "It's me – but me gone mad." Later, at a café, he suddenly threw a glass at Gauguin, who forced him back home and put him to bed. It was the first open sign of the tension between the two artists.

♦ BALLS OF WOOL
Van Gogh used the various-coloured balls of wool in this Japanese box to study the effects of combinations of colour.

PAINTS ♦
Van Gogh used tubes of oil paint, which had been manufactured industrially since 1846. They were easily obtainable and portable, making it possible to work out of doors. They completely replaced the paints that earlier artists had had to prepare themselves.

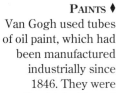

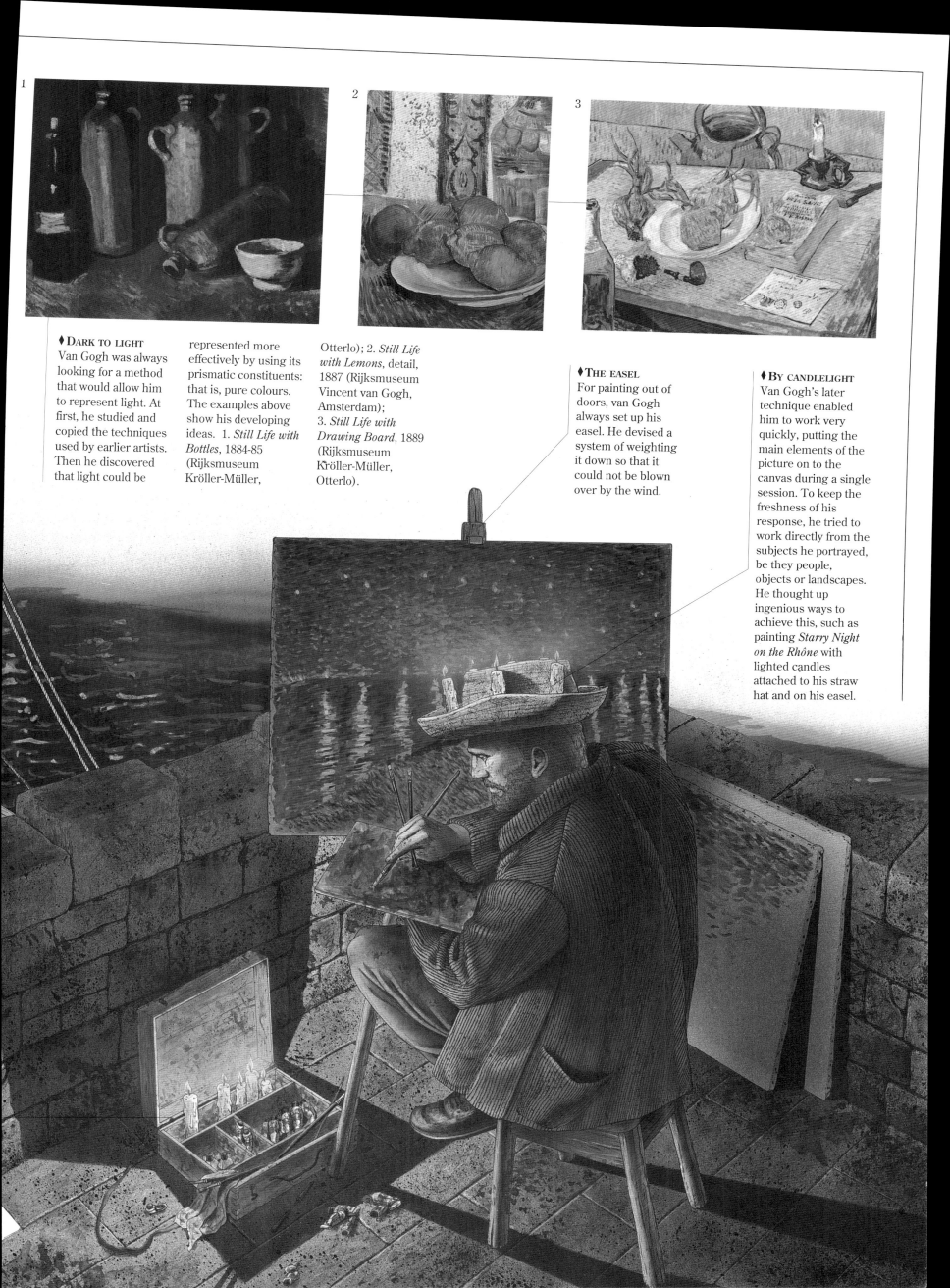

♦ **DARK TO LIGHT**
Van Gogh was always looking for a method that would allow him to represent light. At first, he studied and copied the techniques used by earlier artists. Then he discovered that light could be represented more effectively by using its prismatic constituents: that is, pure colours. The examples above show his developing ideas. 1. *Still Life with Bottles*, 1884-85 (Rijksmuseum Kröller-Müller, Otterlo); 2. *Still Life with Lemons*, detail, 1887 (Rijksmuseum Vincent van Gogh, Amsterdam); 3. *Still Life with Drawing Board*, 1889 (Rijksmuseum Kröller-Müller, Otterlo).

♦ **THE EASEL**
For painting out of doors, van Gogh always set up his easel. He devised a system of weighting it down so that it could not be blown over by the wind.

♦ **BY CANDLELIGHT**
Van Gogh's later technique enabled him to work very quickly, putting the main elements of the picture on to the canvas during a single session. To keep the freshness of his response, he tried to work directly from the subjects he portrayed, be they people, objects or landscapes. He thought up ingenious ways to achieve this, such as painting *Starry Night on the Rhône* with lighted candles attached to his straw hat and on his easel.

THE YELLOW HOUSE

This is a painting of the house that van Gogh rented in Arles, with the intention of turning it into a place where fellow artists could live in a kind of brotherhood, like a medieval guild. The Yellow House stood on the corner of a block of buildings near the station. In one direction, the rue Montmajour led under the railway and out of the city. In the other was the place Lamartine, a three-sided open area. In van Gogh's painting, heaps of earth can be seen on the road and in the area in front of the house.

♦ PLACE LAMARTINE
A drawing by van Gogh of the area in front of the house, 1888 (Rijksmuseum Vincent van Gogh, Amsterdam).

♦ THE WORK
The Yellow House, 1888, oil on canvas, 72 x 91.5 cm (28 x 36 in) (Rijksmuseum Vincent van Gogh, Amsterdam).
Van Gogh painted this work in September 1888, when he had been at Arles for seven months. Having rented the house in May, he had written immediately to Theo: "I enclose a quick sketch on wrapping paper, a grassy area on the [place Lamartine] where you come in to the city, with a house in the background. Well, today I rented the right wing of this house, which has four rooms, or rather two, with two boxrooms. The external walls are painted yellow and inside it is whitewashed, and it gets the sun all day; ... so now I can tell you about my idea to ask Bernard and others to send me their paintings ... at last I will be able to see my paintings in a well-lit environment."

♦ A FIGURE
The man walking along the footpath in front of the house appears in both the oil painting (above) and the watercolour (below).

The colours of Provence soon made their mark on van Gogh's palette: yellow and blue became the colours that he used the most. He used a perspective method that he had already employed in the past: he arranged his picture following a kind of grid of guidelines. The painting of The Yellow House *is built on two diagonals: one on the right gives the effect of depth, tapering off under the railway bridge; the other is the line of the edge of the square. The heaps of earth in the foreground give a sense of distance between the viewer and the house. But the contrasting colours are what count in this painting. "The vault of the sky ... is a magnificent blue; the rays of the sun are a pale sulphur yellow, and this combination of colours is delicate and pleasing."*

♦ A WATERCOLOUR
As well as the oil painting, van Gogh painted this watercolour of *The Yellow House* in September-October 1888 (Rijksmuseum Vincent van Gogh, Amsterdam).

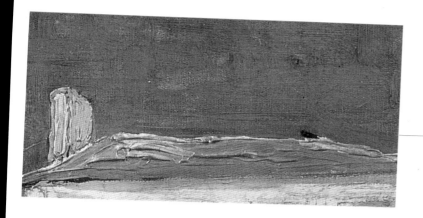

♦ DETAILS
Left: details from *The Yellow House*. The blue of the sky (top) has been created using thick, oily, intensely coloured paint spread with a palette knife. In the yellow light reflected from the walls of the building, daily life goes on peacefully. As well as the customers sitting outside the café (centre), there are people out walking, a mother with her children, and a train (bottom), puffing clouds of smoke, crossing the railway bridge.

♦ AROUND ARLES
Van Gogh arrived in Provence in the middle of winter and found that it was snowing. However, he was still struck by the colours and the light. He could never stop exploring the area. Ignoring the Roman ruins, he went to the banks of the Rhône and to the coast. At the end of June 1888, he painted *Fishing Boats on the Beach at Saintes-Maries* (Rijksmuseum Vincent van Gogh, Amsterdam).

♦ THE HIGH YELLOW NOTE
Yellow – "the high yellow note" that van Gogh said he had found – became one of the colours he used most frequently while he was at Arles. It is the main colour in all the many versions of *Sunflowers* (top: 1889, Rijksmuseum Vincent van Gogh, Amsterdam); and of the above painting of *Haystacks in Provence*, 1888 (Rijksmuseum Kröller-Müller, Otterlo).

PEOPLE OF ARLES

At the end of the nineteenth century, there was a great difference between a capital city with millions of inhabitants and a quiet provincial town.
Physically, Arles was a long train journey away from Paris; but in their lifestyles the two places were even further apart. In Arles, life was based on the principles and values of country life. Van Gogh much preferred the sincerity of the people of Arles to the confusion of Paris. Everyone in the cafés in the evenings knew everyone else, and the skies and colours of Provence were all around to be enjoyed.

♦ THE ROULINS
In mid-August 1888, van Gogh got to know the postal worker Joseph Roulin and his family. He painted many portraits of them while he was in Arles.
Left: *Joseph Roulin*, 1889 (Museum of Fine Arts, Boston).
Left below: *La Berceuse*, 1889 (Private collection). This is a portrait of Joseph's wife holding the cord with which she can rock the baby's cradle.

♦ CAFÉ ALCAZAR
The Yellow House in Arles was destroyed during the Second World War, but the nearby Café Alcazar (above), at number 2 place Lamartine, is still standing today. The café was the subject of one of van Gogh's paintings, which he described in a letter to Theo: "In *The Night Café* I have tried to convey that a café is a place where you can ruin yourself, go mad, commit a crime .... So I have tried to express, as it were, the powers of darkness in a low public house."

IN THE CAFÉ ♦
The café was one of the few meeting-places to go to at the end of a hard day – which, for most people in Arles, meant working in the fields. It was somewhere to drink a glass of wine, eat a hot meal prepared in a back room, and doze off on the table.

12. VAN GOGH'S LIFE ♦ *From Arles, Vincent wrote to Theo: "I am seeing a lot of new things here, I am learning, and my body, if treated with a little kindness, serves me well." He made friends with the Ginoux family and the postal worker Roulin. All the time he painted and, at the end of July, he sent his brother 35 pictures. He kept inviting Paul Gauguin to stay with him and finally, thanks to Theo's intervention and promise to help financially, Gauguin agreed. Van Gogh was excited by his arrival at the Yellow House, but their relationship soon deteriorated. They were opposite personalities: van Gogh tormented, impetuous and untidy, Gauguin apparently self-confident and meticulous. Gauguin found Arles boring and the fear that he might leave put a strain on Vincent.* ⇒•

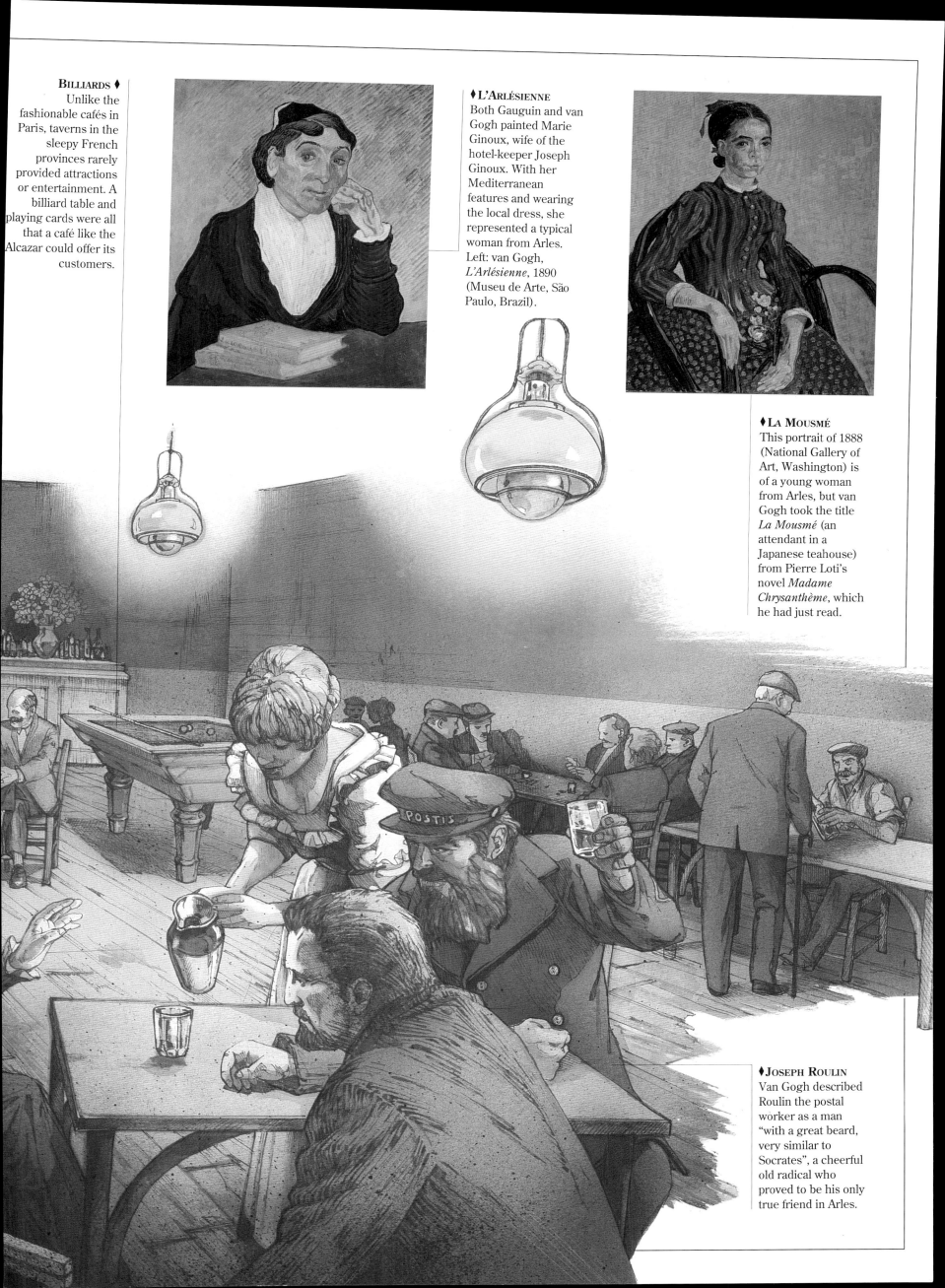

BILLIARDS ♦
Unlike the fashionable cafés in Paris, taverns in the sleepy French provinces rarely provided attractions or entertainment. A billiard table and playing cards were all that a café like the Alcazar could offer its customers.

♦ L'ARLÉSIENNE
Both Gauguin and van Gogh painted Marie Ginoux, wife of the hotel-keeper Joseph Ginoux. With her Mediterranean features and wearing the local dress, she represented a typical woman from Arles. Left: van Gogh, *L'Arlésienne*, 1890 (Museu de Arte, São Paulo, Brazil).

♦ LA MOUSMÉ
This portrait of 1888 (National Gallery of Art, Washington) is of a young woman from Arles, but van Gogh took the title *La Mousmé* (an attendant in a Japanese teahouse) from Pierre Loti's novel *Madame Chrysanthème*, which he had just read.

♦ JOSEPH ROULIN
Van Gogh described Roulin the postal worker as a man "with a great beard, very similar to Socrates", a cheerful old radical who proved to be his only true friend in Arles.

♦ THE WORK
Bedroom in Arles, 1888, oil on canvas, 72 x 90 cm (28 x 35 in) (Rijksmuseum Vincent van Gogh, Amsterdam). The work was painted in October 1888, as we know from a letter bearing that date which van Gogh wrote to Gauguin: "I have painted ... my bedroom, with its ... wood furniture as you know. Well, I really enjoyed doing this stark interior with Seurat-style simplicity. The colours are uniform but applied roughly, without thinning the paint .... I wanted all these different colours to express a totally restful feeling. There is just one dash of white, in the black-framed mirror .... You will see the painting with the others and we can talk about it, because I often don't know what I am doing, since I am working as if I were a sleep-walker." There are two other versions of the painting, both in oils and produced in September 1889. One is at the Musée d'Orsay, Paris, and the other at the Art Institute, Chicago. Above and below are two details from the 1888 version.

BEDROOM IN ARLES

Van Gogh described this painting of his bedroom in the Yellow House, in a letter of 1888: "It is just simply my bedroom .... The walls are pale violet. The floor is covered with red tiles, the wooden bedhead and chairs are as yellow as fresh butter, the sheets and pillows are very pale lemon green. The blanket is scarlet. The window green. The wash-stand is orange and the basin blue. The doors are lilac .... There are some paintings on the wall, a towel and some clothes."

♦ A DRAWING FOR THEO
Vincent described the painting in a letter to Theo in October 1888.

He enclosed the above drawing of it (Rijksmuseum Vincent van Gogh, Amsterdam).

Van Gogh believed that his painting of his bedroom in the Yellow House was a real achievement: he had found a style of his own and a technique of which he felt confident. He produced two replicas of the painting a year later. The technique used in the painting had gone beyond divisionism and Impressionism. The colours were uniform; a palette knife had created broad, flat surfaces; the complementary colours gave an effect of both harmony and energy. Van Gogh had reached a point where his style displayed a considerable degree of freedom. This included freedom from rules of perspective, shown in the arbitrary way in which the surfaces of the table and chair are arranged against the background.

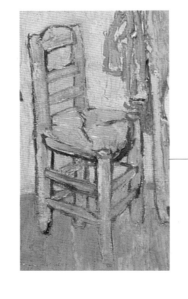

♦ OUTLINES
A detail from *Bedroom in Arles*. Van Gogh was now constructing his compositions using colour – intended both to communicate feelings and to create harmony. However, he still used dark outlines.

♦ **PERSPECTIVE**
In Arles, van Gogh painted some works, like *Bedroom in Arles*, in which the perspective was more or less correct, and others where he treated perspective more freely.

♦ **JUXTAPOSING COLOURS**
This detail from *Bedroom in Arles* shows how van Gogh deliberately paired complementary colours. Here, yellow is placed next to violet, blue with orange, red with green. As Chevreul had pointed out, the effect of juxtaposing complementary colours is that each intensifies the impact of the other. Van Gogh wanted the overall effect of harmony to convey the feeling of "rest", to give a reassuring image of his own daily life.

♦ **PAINTINGS ON THE WALLS**
A detail from *Bedroom in Arles*. Van Gogh's room is shown as simple and tidy and equipped with everyday, basic objects. The paintings on the walls include two portraits (above) and a landscape.

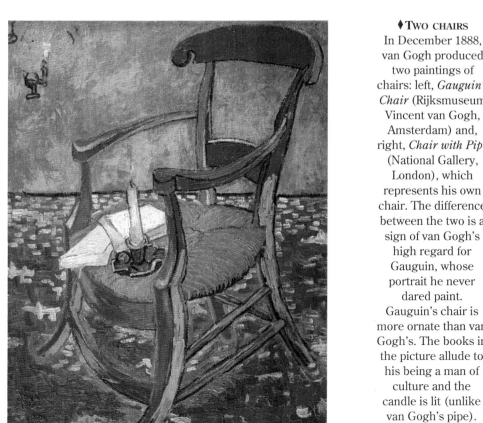

♦ **TWO CHAIRS**
In December 1888, van Gogh produced two paintings of chairs: left, *Gauguin's Chair* (Rijksmuseum Vincent van Gogh, Amsterdam) and, right, *Chair with Pipe* (National Gallery, London), which represents his own chair. The difference between the two is a sign of van Gogh's high regard for Gauguin, whose portrait he never dared paint. Gauguin's chair is more ornate than van Gogh's. The books in the picture allude to his being a man of culture and the candle is lit (unlike van Gogh's pipe).

GAUGUIN

Like van Gogh, Paul Gauguin was an artist for long misunderstood, who suffered and struggled as he developed his ideas and became a great innovator. He broke away from Impressionism to work in a new style, Synthetism, which he and Emile Bernard developed together. Because of his strong personality and mature age, he became an influence on many young painters.

♦ **VASE WITH BRETON SCENES**
Ceramic, 29 cm (11½ in) high, 1887-88 (Musée Royaux d'Art et d'Histoire, Brussels).

♦ **HIS LIFE**
Paul Gauguin was born in Paris in 1848, but spent his childhood in Lima, Peru, as well as in the French cities of Rouen and Orléans. He joined the merchant marines, travelling around the world, and then worked as a stockbroker in Paris. Meanwhile Pissarro was encouraging him to paint, and he began to adopt the style and techniques of the Impressionists. When he lost his job in 1883, he decided to devote himself entirely to painting. This was the start of a troubled life marked by a need to escape and explore. He left his wife and children and moved to Brittany, then to Panama and Martinique, then back to Pont-Aven in Brittany, to Arles to stay with van Gogh, to Brittany again, and finally to Tahiti and the Marquesas Islands. In Polynesia he hoped that he had finally found the paradise on earth that he had sought: a simple, untainted and primitive place. In all the tumult of his artistic activity, Gauguin found time not only for painting but also for sculpture, ceramics and writing. He died in 1903 in the Marquesas Islands.

♦ **A SELF-PORTRAIT VASE**
1889 (Kunstindustrimuseet, Copenhagen). Gauguin began to produce ceramics in 1886. Often, as in this example, he took his inspiration from Inca terracotta work seen in his childhood in Peru.

♦ **TO HIS FRIEND VINCENT**
Shortly before going to stay with Vincent van Gogh in Arles, Gauguin painted this *Self-portrait (Les Misérables)*, 1888 (Rijksmuseum Vincent van Gogh, Amsterdam). He wrote about the painting in a letter, remarking that the artist looks like "a powerful and roughly-dressed bandit".

♦ **THE FIRST TAHITIAN PORTRAIT**
Vahine no te Tiare (Woman with Flower), 1891 (Ny Carlsberg Glyptotek, Copenhagen), was the first portrait of a native woman that Gauguin painted in Polynesia. He must have been annoyed to find that the girl insisted on being painted in her Sunday best dress. Later he made most of his models wear the pre-colonial *pareo* (wrap-around skirt).

THE SAVAGE ♦
Oviri, 1894 (Musée d'Orsay, Paris). Gauguin produced this ceramic in Paris, after his first trip to Polynesia. The title *Oviri* means "savage" – an adjective that Gauguin liked to apply to himself. In Polynesia, he found the primitive dimension he had been searching for during his stays in Brittany. The primitive art of Africa and Oceania would later inspire artists like Picasso.

◆ **PARADISE ON EARTH**
Gauguin arrived in Tahiti for the first time in June 1891, after a sea voyage lasting almost three months. He had raised the money for the trip by auctioning his paintings.
Left: *Nevermore*, 1894 (Courtauld Institute Galleries, London). When he painted this, Gauguin had committed himself to spend the rest of his life in Polynesia. It conveys the sense of mystery that he found in these enchanting islands.

◆ **THE PONT-AVEN SCHOOL**
Clear outlines, large areas of juxtaposed complementary colours, no shading, no attempt to convey a sense of depth, and a very free representation of reality: these were the principles that inspired a group of painters who gathered in the Breton village of Pont-Aven. Their leader from 1888 was Gauguin, but other important members were Paul Sérusier and Maxime Maufra. Above: a detail from Sérusier's *The Talisman*, 1888 (Musée d'Orsay, Paris). Above right: Maufra, *Landscape at Pont-Aven*, 1890 (Musée des Beaux-Arts, Quimper).

SYNTHETISM ◆
The sacred, the primitive and the mysterious had already appeared in Gauguin's paintings during his Breton period. *Jacob's Struggle with the Angel* (right), 1888 (National Gallery of Scotland, Edinburgh), is an example. Gauguin broke away from naturalism to develop a simplified style that would convey the essence of things (Synthetism). He recommended painting from memory, rather than from objects in front of the artist. In this he differed from van Gogh, whose works were usually painted from reality.

STARRY NIGHT

In painting this scene, van Gogh was probably combining real and imaginary, Provençal and northern elements, and so it has been suggested that he was remembering Holland in the village on the right. But, there have been various interpretations of *Starry Night*. It may be a representation, in van Gogh's most visionary style, of the sky in June 1889, expressing emotions inexpressible in any other medium; but another suggestion is that the galactic turbulence is a symbol for Christ's Passion.

♦ THE CHURCH TOWER
A detail from *Starry Night*. The sleeping village with its little church plays a distinctly secondary role compared with the spectacle of the starry sky.

♦ THE WORK
Starry Night, 1889, oil on canvas, 73.7 x 92.1 cm (29 x 36 in) (Museum of Modern Art, New York). Van Gogh worked on this painting in June 1889, at the mental hospital in Saint-Rémy to which he had admitted himself the previous month. At this time, he was particularly interested in cypress trees, writing: "I constantly think about cypresses. I would like to do something with them as I did with the pictures of sunflowers, for I am amazed that they have not been done in the way I see them. The line and proportions of a cypress resemble those of an Egyptian obelisk." The hospital allowed van Gogh to go out during the day with his canvases, easel and paints. The subjects he found to paint were dry-stone walls, hills, villages, olive trees and cypresses. The village in *Starry Night* could be Saint-Rémy, with some changes made, especially to the church tower, to give it a northern feel.

♦ STUDIES OF THE SWIRLS
The above drawing dated 1889 (Kunsthalle, Bremen) shows how carefully van Gogh studied – line by line – each individual swirl that makes up the image. Often painstaking preparatory work is done to produce a painting that looks spontaneous.

♦ THE STARS
A detail from *Starry Night*. A few yellow and white brush-strokes on a blue background make the stars burst open like flares.

While he was in the hospital at Saint-Rémy, van Gogh alternated between periods of hyperactivity and long spells of deep depression. His altered state of mind was reflected in a change in his style of painting. During the time he spent in Arles, his work had been characterized by the use of pure colours, uniformly spread in large areas. At Saint-Rémy, however, grey, ochre and blended colours made their appearance again. These were much the same colours as he had used for his paintings in Nuenen, but he used lighter tones of them now. Another change was that the energy previously expressed in colour made itself felt, instead, in the lines in the painting. They twisted and turned, writhed, flared and became grouped in great swirls, filling the canvas with movement. The result was a dynamic style of painting in which the artist's inner turmoil was projected on to the world.

♦ VAN GOGH'S SYMBOLISM
A detail from *Starry Night*. Some critics have suggested that van Gogh meant to do more than represent the world in a naturalistic way and that he included certain elements in his paintings as symbols, to communicate a more complex message. Seen from this point of view, the cypress tree in the left-hand foreground of *Starry Night*, linking the earth with the sky, could be understood as a symbol of death.

♦ **NOCTURNAL SCENES**
For some time van Gogh had been trying to show that the night, like the day, is full of colours that artists should capture rather than painting with the usual blacks.
Left: *Café Terrace at Night*, complete and detail, 1888 (Rijksmuseum Kröller-Müller, Otterlo).
Below: *Starry Night on the Rhône*, detail, 1888 (Musée d'Orsay, Paris).

♦ **THE MOVING LINE**
A new style emerged in van Gogh's painting after the period in Arles and while he was in hospital at Saint-Rémy. It can be seen in *Starry Night* and in other paintings of this time. Instead of the large, luminous areas of pure colour that characterized his earlier paintings, van Gogh now used long brush-strokes to create undulating movement across the whole canvas. Both *The Alpilles with Olive Trees*, above (Private collection), and *Cypresses*, right (Metropolitan Museum of Art, New York), were painted in Saint-Rémy in June 1889.

THE ASYLUM

Nineteenth-century lunatic asylums (or, as they are now more often called, mental hospitals) varied in the treatment they offered. Patients might find themselves forcibly restrained, or in the care of enthusiastic experimenters, or even in the hands of eccentric charlatans. For a long time, most asylums had born a close resemblance to prisons. Mental illness was only ever handled humanely if the patient had some social status or if he or she was fortunate enough to find a sympathetic doctor. However, towards the end of the century, a new, scientific approach to mental disorders was taking form. In 1885, a young Viennese doctor, Sigmund Freud, went to meet the famous neurologist Jean-Martin Charcot at the Salpêtrière hospital in Paris. Charcot's influence was important in Freud's evolution into the father of psychoanalysis and in the beginning of the new approach to mental illness. In 1889, van Gogh admitted himself to the asylum at Saint-Rémy in Provence. The living conditions he found there were better than average for the time.

♦ **DR REY**
Van Gogh was fortunate to meet understanding doctors like Dr Félix Rey, who worked at the Arles hospital. Later, his life at the Saint-Rémy asylum was quiet and calm. Theo paid for Vincent's room and board at this private institution. Patients were left to their own devices, the only treatment being hydrotherapeutic bathing.
Left: Van Gogh, *Portrait of Dr Rey*, 1889 (Pushkin Museum, Moscow).

♦ **AT ARLES**
At the hospital in Arles, when he was not resting or talking with Dr Rey, van Gogh drew and painted other patients and the hospital itself.
Left: *Courtyard of the Arles Hospital*, April 1889 (Oskar Reinhart Collection, Winterthur).

♦ **FREUD**
A young Viennese doctor, Sigmund Freud, the future father of psychoanalysis, was present at Professor Charcot's lectures.

13. VAN GOGH'S LIFE ♦ *It became clear that van Gogh and Gauguin could not live together. They had many arguments and, according to Gauguin, on 23 December 1888, Vincent followed his friend into the street and threatened him with a razor. On the same night, he cut off his own earlobe, wrapped it in newspaper and took it to Rachel, a prostitute in a nearby brothel. Next morning the police found him unconscious in his bed at the Yellow House. He was taken to the Arles hospital, but his recovery was short-lived and the local people turned against him. On 8 May 1889 van Gogh admitted himself to the Saint-Paul-de-Mausole asylum, near Saint-Rémy. Here Dr Peyron diagnosed epilepsy and van Gogh seemed to be improving. He could paint, draw and talk to the other patients. Then, in July, he had another serious attack, during which he swallowed some paint.* ➡➔

◆THE CUT EAR
Van Gogh cut off his own earlobe after an argument with Gauguin in the Yellow House on 23 December 1888. Despite this complete breakdown, van Gogh seemed to recover quickly. Left: *A Self-portrait* of January 1889 (Courtauld Institute Galleries, London) shows how van Gogh saw himself at this time, with his ear bandaged.

◆STRAITJACKETS
In the nineteenth century and long after, a mentally ill person was often strapped into a straitjacket.

◆TREATING THE MENTALLY ILL
Dr Rey was not a specialist but had the good sense to advise van Gogh not to drink. On the other hand, Dr Théophile Peyron, the director of the hospital at Saint-Rémy, was laxer in his treatment. For example, he did not forbid alcohol; in fact, van Gogh described his system sarcastically: "It must be easy to treat the sick here: absolutely nothing is done for them."
Before Freud and the development of psychoanalysis, methods of treating the insane and studies of the mind and its neuroses were very rudimentary. There was a fashionable belief in the importance of measurable physiological factors. Insanity and criminal tendencies were thought to reveal themselves in certain aspects of a person's physical appearance. It was believed that by measuring the capacity of the cranium and by interpreting physical attributes, it was possible to control, predict and combat crime. However, Jean-Martin Charcot (1825-1893) laid the foundations for modern neuropathology during this period. He lectured in Paris, at the Sorbonne and, from 1882, at the Salpêtrière. A photograph of him is shown at the top of this column.

◆CHARCOT AT THE SALPÊTRIÈRE
Professor Jean-Martin Charcot gave his lectures on hypnosis as a treatment for hysteria, at the Salpêtrière. This prestigious university building had formerly been an asylum for mentally ill women. Humane methods of treatment had first been tried out there during the French Revolution.

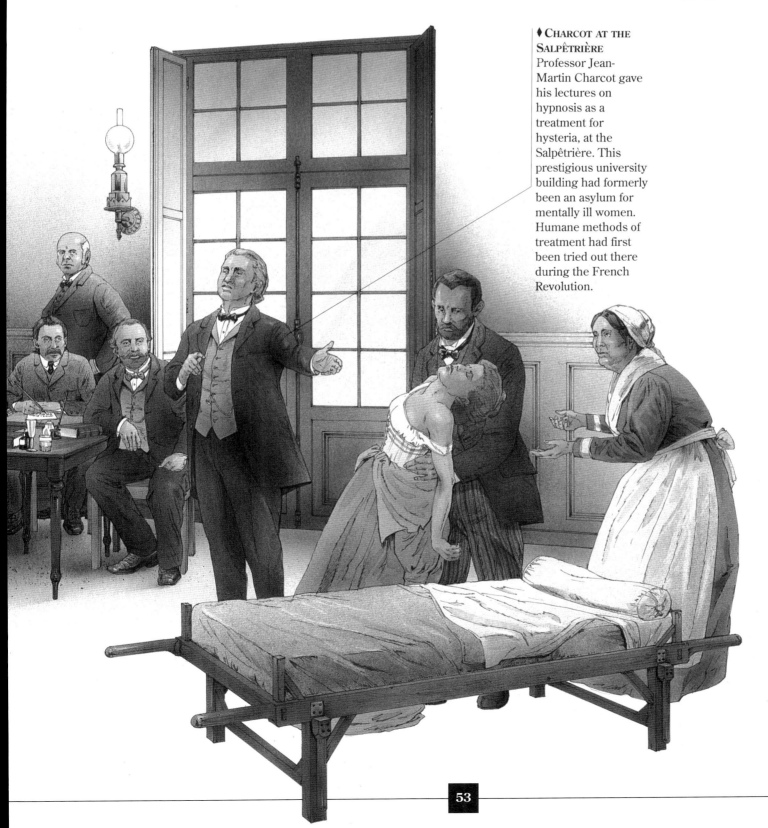

DOCTOR GACHET

Doctor Paul Gachet, a friend of artists and an artist himself, took care of van Gogh during the period when he was living in the town of Auvers. In one of his letters, van Gogh described how he was painting the doctor: "I am working on his portrait, he is wearing a white cap, he is very blond, very fair, even the skin on his hands is pinkish, a blue suit and a cobalt blue background; he is leaning on a red table."

♦ **DR GACHET IN 1890**
This photograph shows Paul Gachet at the age of sixty-two, at the time when he and van Gogh were friends.

♦ **THE WORK**
Portrait of Dr Gachet, June 1890, oil on canvas, 68 x 57 cm (27 x 22½ in) (Musée d'Orsay, Paris). Van Gogh painted this portrait, and several others of the doctor and members of his family, on one of the many occasions that he visited Gachet during May and June 1890. "Nothing, absolutely nothing could keep me here except Gachet," he wrote to his brother Theo. "I always feel that I can work quite easily in his house, every time I go there, and he always asks me to lunch either on Sundays or Mondays." Paul-Ferdinand Gachet (1828-1909) had studied medicine in Paris but, while he was still a student, he had become interested in art and had been in contact with Gustave Courbet and his followers. After he moved to Auvers, outside the capital, he still kept a clinic open in Paris. He was a socialist and a Darwinian, and became a defender of modern artists, especially Cézanne and Pissarro. An artist himself and good at drawing, he introduced van Gogh to etching.

♦ **IN AND AROUND AUVERS**
At Auvers, van Gogh experienced a short, peaceful period of working calmly. The town, its surroundings and its inhabitants all became part of the world of his paintings.
Left: *Dr Gachet's Garden in Auvers*, May 1890 (Musée d'Orsay, Paris).

♦ **PORTRAITS, NOT PHOTOGRAPHS**
Van Gogh created three portraits of his friend Paul Gachet. Above: *Portrait of Gachet with Pipe*, etching, May 1890 (Rijksmuseum Kröller-Müller, Otterlo). The artist described his plans for these pictures: "I would like to make these portraits so that they seem like living presences to people who see them in a hundred years from now. I am trying to achieve this, not by producing photographic likenesses, but by empathetic expression" – that is, by trying to feel what the person is feeling, in order to express his or her soul, or essence, in the painting.

While he was in Auvers, van Gogh seems to have tried to keep his imagination under control. The twisting, swirling, emphatic lines of the paintings he had produced in Saint-Rémy now disappeared from his work. They were replaced by an approach that was much calmer and more reflective, showing a new desire for order and tranquillity. The portrait of Gachet shows the doctor's melancholy nature. Van Gogh wrote that the face had "the heart-broken expression of our time".

♦ **ANOTHER VERSION**
In June 1890 van Gogh painted this second version in oils of the portrait of Gachet (Private collection). Here we can see traces of the artist's Saint-Rémy style, with swarms of small brush-strokes following the contours.

♦ THE EYES AND THE SOUL
A detail from *Portrait of Dr Gachet*. Van Gogh tried to get right inside his subject's mind, in order to be able to portray his inner being, or soul. He saw the doctor as a melancholy, thoughtful man, and wrote about him to his sister: "I have found a true friend in Gachet. He is something like a brother, we resemble each other physically and spiritually as well, he is also nervous and odd ... like you and me. He is older and has been a widower for a few years, but he is a doctor through and through, and his faith and vocation give him the strength to carry on."

♦ THE LAST PORTRAIT
This was the last portrait made of Vincent van Gogh. It was drawn as he lay on his deathbed, on 29 July 1890, by his friend and doctor, Paul Gachet (Musée d'Orsay, Paris).

THE FOXGLOVE ♦
In painting the stem of foxglove in Gachet's hand, van Gogh was making a deliberate reference to the doctor's profession. Gachet was a homoeopathic doctor who used plants in his medicines.

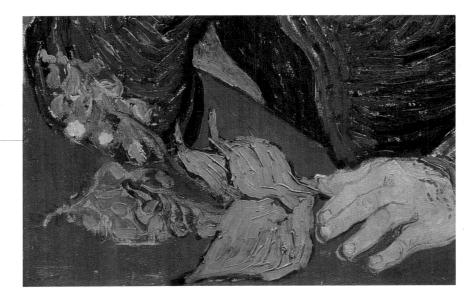

♦ DR GACHET AND CÉZANNE
In 1873, Dr Gachet had persuaded Paul Cézanne to come to Auvers. Several paintings and engravings by Cézanne date from the time he spent there.
Left: Cézanne, *Dr Gachet in the Studio*, 1873 (Musée d'Orsay, Paris).
Right: Cézanne, *Dr Gachet's House at Auvers*, 1873 (Musée d'Orsay, Paris).

THE ART MARKET

Today, van Gogh's paintings fetch the highest prices at auctions around the world, but in his lifetime he sold only one painting. Not everyone was so unlucky. Other painters did better and some of them became quite wealthy. Still, in late-nineteenth-century France, it was an uphill struggle for artists who did not paint in the style approved by dominant institutions such as the Salon and the academies. They spent their lives in temporary lodgings, often in poverty, finding it difficult to sell their work unless they found wealthy and enlightened patrons. Even in the twentieth century, it was from such humble studios, usually in the district of Montmartre, that painters like Picasso and Modigliani emerged.

♦ **THE FIRST DEALERS**
While conventional artists could count on public and private purchasers for their work, the innovative Impressionist painters had to rely on dealers, speculators and a few wealthy patrons with advanced tastes. This was the beginning of the modern free market in works of art. Many early buyers of Impressionist paintings were businessmen and professionals (including many doctors, like Gachet). There were a few professional dealers, such as Paul Durand-Ruel, but most were shopkeepers or restauranteurs who accepted paintings, instead of money, in payment of bills, and often had no clear idea of the value of the works that came into their possession in this way. Among such people were the confectioner Eugène Murer, the margarine manufacturer Auguste Pellerin, the mattress-maker Père Soulier, and also second-hand dealers, picture framers and sellers of artists' materials such as Père Tanguy. One pioneering dealer who recognized the value of the new artists was Ambroise Vollard, originally a notary. His photograph appears at the top of this column. For just a few francs, he bought the paintings that Theo van Gogh left behind at the Boussod and Valadon gallery. These included many works by Vincent and some by Gauguin.

♦ **A MEAL AT A TAVERN**
Above: van Gogh, *La Guinguette* (a tavern in Montmartre), 1886 (Rijksmuseum Vincent van Gogh, Amsterdam). During the 1880s, the average monthly wage of an office worker in Paris was 125 francs. A meal at a tavern in Montmartre cost 90 centimes. Painters sometimes paid with one of their canvases.

14. VAN GOGH'S LIFE ♦ *In summer 1889, van Gogh had a serious mental collapse at Saint-Rémy, but his letters show that his intermittent attacks did not prevent him from expressing himself with exceptional lucidity and awareness, even about his own condition. Although for part of the time he was at his worst, medically speaking, at Saint-Rémy he produced 150 paintings and, as Emile Bernard wrote, "perhaps he had never painted so well". Meanwhile, Theo van Gogh had married Johanna Bonger, the sister of a friend, in Amsterdam in April 1889. He agreed that his brother should move to Auvers-sur-Oise, just outside Paris, where Dr Gachet could supervise him.* ≫

♦ **VAN GOGH'S ONLY SALE**
The Red Vineyard, painted at Arles in November 1888 (Pushkin Museum, Moscow), was the only painting that van Gogh sold during his lifetime.

♦ **RECORD AUCTIONS**
Van Gogh wrote sadly about his own problems in trying to achieve any success in selling his work. The only painting he ever sold, *The Red Vineyard*, was bought by the sister of his friend, the poet Eugène Boch. And Theo van Gogh encountered great difficulties trying to get his brother's work appreciated and its value recognized. All these facts make it bitterly ironical that a painting by van Gogh has since become the most expensive work ever to be sold. The *Portrait of Dr Gachet* of 1890, once in the Metropolitan Museum of Art in New York, was sold at auction in that city on 15 May 1990 for $82,500,000. Three years before, van Gogh's *Irises*, 1889 (left, Paul Getty Museum, Malibu, California), had been sold for $53,900,000, also in New York.

THE AUCTIONEER ♦
At an auction, the auctioneer is responsible for knocking down (that is, selling) every lot. He bangs his gavel on his desk to indicate that the bidding is over.

THE NOTICE-BOARD ♦
Nowadays a notice-board displays updated information on the prices fetched by objects in the auction, with the equivalent amounts shown in the principal currencies.

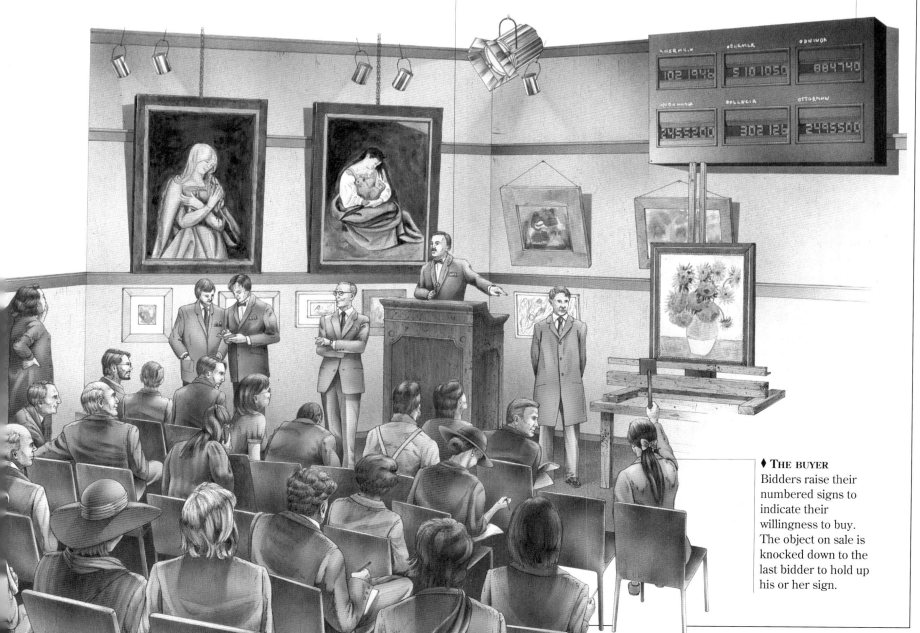

♦ **THE BUYER**
Bidders raise their numbered signs to indicate their willingness to buy. The object on sale is knocked down to the last bidder to hold up his or her sign.

THE CHURCH AT AUVERS

♦ **DETAILS**
Above and below: details of *The Church at Auvers*: the clock on the bell-tower and the tracery of a window.

♦ **THE WORK**
The Church at Auvers, June 1890, oil on canvas, 94 x 74 cm (37 x 29 in) (Musée d'Orsay, Paris). In the two months that he spent in Auvers, van Gogh produced about eighty paintings: more than one a day. He was active, he had stopped drinking and he had rediscovered the pleasure of painting outdoors. The subjects he chose were children, landscapes, portraits and the houses of the confectioner and of Daubigny (1817-1878), a painter of the Barbizon school who had lived in Auvers after leaving the Forest of Fontainebleau. By painting, van Gogh was trying to find a way out of the obsessions that had tormented him in recent months. The church of Notre-Dame is a twelfth- and thirteenth-century structure, built in a mixture of Romanesque and Gothic styles. Van Gogh's painting of it is one of his most highly-regarded and best-known works.

Van Gogh described this painting in a letter to his sister Wilhelmina: "A large painting of the village church, executed so that the building appears purplish against a sky which is the deep and simple blue of pure cobalt; the windows seem stained with ultramarine; the roof is part violet, part orange. In front, there are flowers growing in the grass and some sunny, pink sand."

♦ **THE CHURCH TODAY**
The Romanesque-Gothic church of Notre-Dame, still the principal church in Auvers today.

♦ **THE TOWN HALL**
Van Gogh witnessed the life of Auvers. Above is a detail from *The Town Hall on 14 July*, 1890 (Private collection). The building had been decorated with flags for the anniversary of the storming of the Bastille – symbol of the beginning of the French Revolution.

♦ **DAUBIGNY'S GARDEN**
Below: Van Gogh, *The Garden of Daubigny's House*, 1890 (Öffentliche Kunstsammlung, Basel). Daubigny was an artist of the Barbizon school who lived in Auvers.

This is one of the canvases painted during the last two months of van Gogh's life, when he was attempting to combine the sometimes violent expression of his own inner turmoil with the kind of balance and integration normally characteristic of a finished work of art. As a result, the paintings are remarkably varied in mood and technique, swinging abruptly from agitation to serenity.

♦ **LIGHT COLOURS, FLOWING LINES**
Left and right: details from *The Church at Auvers*. When van Gogh lived at Auvers, his palette became more colourful than ever. He still used strong contours, along with dynamic brush-strokes that flowed along them.

♦ **FREEDOM FROM PERSPECTIVE**
Left: a detail from *The Church at Auvers*. As you look at many works by van Gogh, it becomes clear that he has ignored the rules of linear perspective used to create a three-dimensional effect in the two-dimensional mediums of painting and drawing. For van Gogh, lines were not a means to imitate the kind of physical space seen in reality, but enabled him to impose his inner vision on the outside world.

WHEAT AND CROWS ♦
Van Gogh's troubled search for harmony at Auvers frequently gave way to tension and turbulence. It has often been suggested that there is a link between the agitated brush-strokes in *Wheatfield with Crows*, July 1890 (Rijks-museum Vincent van Gogh, Amsterdam), and the artist's imminent suicide, of which the black birds are seen as an omen.

♦ **A CORNER OF AUVERS**
Above: *Street and Steps in Auvers, with Figures*, late May 1890 (Saint Louis Art Museum, Saint Louis). In the two months that he spent at Auvers, van Gogh immersed himself in country life, producing paintings full of vitality, like the one shown here. They were brightly coloured and often included human figures.

EXPRESSIONISM

Van Gogh did not have pupils or followers, and did not create a school of painting. He was a solitary genius, a loner, even though he could count on the esteem of a small number of fellow artists. Yet he made a fundamental contribution to the later development of modern art. The influence of his ideas and method of painting are most obvious in the works of the twentieth-century Expressionists, from the Fauves and the Die Brücke group to Edvard Munch.

♦ **HENRI MATISSE**
Matisse (1869-1954) was the leader of a group of artists whose work was characterized by their search for an emotional relationship with nature. In 1905 their first exhibition in Paris caused a scandal; they were named "Fauves" – wild beasts.
Left: *View of Collioure*, 1905 (Hermitage, St Petersburg).

♦ **VAN GOGH'S EXPRESSIONISM**
Van Gogh sought to convey the inner nature of things rather than merely representing the visible world. His expressive ability was noticed in 1890 by the critic, Albert Aurier: "His whole work is excessive: excess of strength, nervousness, expressive violence." The Expressionists took up this aspect of van Gogh's work.
Above: *Wheatfield with Crows,* detail, 1890 (Rijksmuseum Vincent van Gogh, Amsterdam).

♦ **ANDRÉ DERAIN**
One of the Fauves was the French painter, André Derain (1880-1954), a friend of Matisse and especially of Vlaminck. Later, he became a follower of Cézanne and a theoretician of Cubism. He moved away from the frenzy of pure colour in his earlier work to more calm and reflective compositions which, especially after the First World War in which he fought as a soldier, showed the influence of the old masters such as the Italian Caravaggio (1571-1610).
Right: *Landscape at Collioure*, complete and detail, 1905 (National Gallery of Art, Washington). It is obvious from this painting that Derain's early style was influenced by the Expressionist outlook and, above all, by the paintings of van Gogh.

15. VAN GOGH'S LIFE ♦ *1890 started well. Theo sold one of his brother's paintings,* The Red Vineyard. *Vincent's move to Auvers in May and his friendship with Dr Gachet seemed to restore some calm to his life. In the next two months he produced about eighty paintings. In July, however, he was worried by Theo's financial difficulties. His letters reveal his bitter feelings about art dealers and a state of affairs in which a dead artist was valued more than a living one. On 27 July, he went out to paint, and after he returned that evening, M et Mme Ravoux, with whom he lodged, discovered that he had shot himself with a revolver. Dr Gachet came at once and Theo was called to Vincent's bedside. Vincent died on 29 July, after spending the day smoking his pipe and talking with his brother. Theo died on 25 January 1891 and was eventually buried next to Vincent in Auvers.*

♦ **ERNST LUDWIG KIRCHNER**
This German painter (1880-1938) was the driving force behind the group called Die Brücke, which he founded in 1905. These painters used colour in a non-naturalistic way and distorted their subjects, to give their works a strong emotional impact. Left *Woman in a Birch Wood*, 1906 (Thyssen Foundation, Madrid).

♦ MAURICE DE VLAMINCK
This French artist (1876-1958) began to paint in 1901, after seeing a van Gogh exhibition.
Left and right: *Houses and Trees*, complete and detail, 1906 (Metropolitan Museum of Art, New York). This shows Vlaminck's non-naturalistic, expressive use of pure colour.

♦ ERICH HECKEL
Having studied architecture, Heckel (1883-1970) took up painting because of his fascination with the work of Edvard Munch and Vincent van Gogh. With Kirchner, in Dresden in 1905, he was one of the founders of the group known as Die Brücke. The work of these painters represented one extreme of German Expressionism. At the other extreme was the "spiritual" art of the Blaue Reiter group. Heckel's Expressionism is marked by a strong streak of aggression and, particularly just before the outbreak of the First World War, a feeling of anxiety. His style, like that of the other members of Die Brücke, is harsh, bold and full of emotional violence.
Left: Erich Heckel, *Brickwork*, 1907 (Thyssen Foundation, Madrid).

♦ EMIL NOLDE
Nolde (1867-1956) began work designing and carving furniture. Then, influenced by van Gogh, Gauguin and Munch, he turned to painting. For a time he was a member of the Die Brücke group, and took his inspiration from primitive art, old carvings and the colours in van Gogh's work.
Right: *In the Wheat*, 1906 (Nolde Foundation, Seebüll).

♦ EDVARD MUNCH
This Norwegian painter (1863-1944) travelled a great deal in France, Italy and Germany. He was influenced by the Impressionists, Gauguin and van Gogh. His own Expressionist style is based on the use of colour to create unreal, anguished and highly dramatic scenes.
Right: *Starry Night*, 1924-25 (Munch Museet, Oslo).

◆ KEY DATES IN VAN GOGH'S LIFE

1853	Vincent Willem van Gogh was born on 30 March in the Dutch village of Groot Zundert. He was the eldest of six children of Theodorus, a Protestant minister, and Anna Cornelia Carbentus.
1857	His brother, Theo, was born on 1 May. A close bond developed between the two brothers and greatly influenced both their lives.
1869	In August Vincent began work at The Hague branch of Goupil and Co., Paris art dealers.
1873	Theo was also employed by Goupil's, in the Brussels branch. In May, Vincent was transferred to London where he stayed for about two years.
1875	Vincent was moved to the Goupil head office in Paris, but he neglected his duties as he became more and more deeply religious.
1876	Having been dismissed on 1 April, Vincent went to England as a teacher. In December, he returned to live with his parents who had moved to Etten.
1878	Wishing to become a lay preacher, Vincent enrolled in an evangelical training school near Brussels, but failed the course. At the end of the year, he went to the southern Belgian mining region of the Borinage, to preach and care for the poor and sick.
1880	Vincent moved to Brussels, where he met the Dutch painter Anton van Rappard. Theo was now sending him a little money.
1885	Vincent was living with his parents in Nuenen, where he produced many pictures of the peasant community, when his father died in March 1885. In November he moved to the Belgian city of Antwerp, where he enrolled in the Art Academy.
1886	Turned down for further study at the Antwerp Art Academy, Vincent went to Paris. He lived with Theo, who was now running the Boussod and Valadon gallery. At the Cormon atelier he met the artists Bernard, Toulouse-Lautrec and Anquetin.
1887	Vincent went often to Asnières, on the outskirts of Paris, where he and Bernard painted "en plein air" on the banks of the Seine.
1888	Vincent moved from Paris to Arles, in Provence, where he rented a wing of the Yellow House with the intention of setting up an artists' colony. He made friends with café owners Joseph and Marie Ginoux and with a postal worker, Joseph Roulin, and painted many portraits of them. In October, Paul Gauguin arrived to stay at the Yellow House. After an argument with him on 23 December, Vincent cut off his own earlobe and took it to a prostitute he knew in a nearby brothel. The next morning he was found unconscious in his bed and was taken to the Arles hospital.
1889	On 8 May, Vincent admitted himself to the Saint-Paul-de-Mausole asylum, near Saint-Rémy. In July, he had another serious attack, during which he swallowed some paint.
1890	Vincent moved to Auvers, just outside Paris, where he became friendly with Dr Paul Gachet. On 27 July, while out painting, he shot himself with a revolver. Gachet called Theo, who went immediately to his brother's bedside. Vincent died two days later on 29 July.
1891	Theo died on 25 January, six months after Vincent's death. He was eventually buried in the Auvers cemetery, next to his brother's grave.

◆ WHERE TO SEE WORKS BY VAN GOGH

Van Gogh's works can be found in museums and private collections throughout the world, including in Russia, France, Germany, the United States and Japan. However, the two major collections of his works are in his native Holland: in the Rijksmuseum Vincent van Gogh in Amsterdam and the Rijksmuseum Kröller-Müller in Otterlo. Works that were kept for many years by Johanna Bonger, the wife of Theo van Gogh, and their son Vincent are also now housed in the Amsterdam museum. In addition to drawings and paintings, it exhibits family photographs and the letters that Vincent and Theo exchanged. A fair number of works by van Gogh can be found in other Dutch museums such as the Stedelijk Museum in Amsterdam, the Boymans-van Beuningen Museum in Rotterdam and the Haag Gemeentemuseum in The Hague. Outside Holland, the Musée d'Orsay in Paris, the Metropolitan Museum of Art in New York and the Chicago Art Institute also contain large collections of van Gogh's work.

AMSTERDAM

RIJKSMUSEUM VINCENT VAN GOGH
The Dutch government has devoted this museum entirely to the life and works of Vincent van Gogh. Here can be seen his portraits of the peasant people drawn and painted during the Nuenen period; his still lifes, such as *Still Life with a Plate of Lemons* and *Still Life with Bread*; the views of Paris, including *Vegetable Gardens in Montmartre* and *Boulevard de Clichy*; and many self-portraits. Other works found here include *Worshippers Leaving the Church at Nuenen*, *Gauguin's Chair*, a version of *The Potato Eaters* (the other is in Otterlo), *Skull with Lit Cigarette*, *The Langlois Bridge*, *Wheatfield with Crows*.

OTTERLO

RIJKSMUSEUM KRÖLLER-MÜLLER
This museum began with a large donation of works from a Dutch collector. Paintings here include some from the Nuenen period: a series showing weavers at their looms, the heads of Brabant peasant people, and the other version of *The Potato Eaters*. There are works from van Gogh's Paris period, such as *Moulin de la Galette*, *Windmills in Montmartre*, *Interior of a Restaurant*; works he painted in Arles, including *Pink Peach Tree in Blossom*, *The Langlois Bridge with Women Washing*, *Haystacks in Provence*, *Café Terrace at Night*; works from Saint-Rémy, such as *Landscape with Rising Moon* and a version of *L'Arlésienne*; and works produced in Auvers, such as *Landscape with Three Trees and Houses* and *Haystack on a Rainy Day*.

PARIS

MUSÉE D'ORSAY
The Musée d'Orsay has over twenty works by van Gogh, representing most stages of the artist's career. They include self-portraits from 1887 and 1889, *Starry Night on the Rhône*, a version of *Bedroom in Arles*, one of *L'Arlésienne* and the painting of *Dr Gachet's Garden at Auvers*.

NEW YORK

METROPOLITAN MUSEUM OF ART
The works exhibited here include *Peasant Woman Peeling Potatoes* and *Peasant Woman Seated in front of the Stove*, both painted in Nuenen in 1885; *Two Cut Sunflowers*, dated 1887; *Self-portrait with Straw Hat*, painted during the winter of 1887-88; one of the many portraits of Marie Ginoux and a portrait of Joseph Roulin, both from the Arles period.

CHICAGO

THE ART INSTITUTE
This museum houses another of van Gogh's self-portraits, painted in Paris during the spring of 1887, *Still Life with Grapes, Apples, Lemons and Pear*, *La Berceuse* (a portrait of Mme Roulin), a *View of the Park at Arles* and a version of *Bedroom in Arles*.

♦ LIST OF WORKS INCLUDED IN THIS BOOK

The works reproduced in this book are listed here, with (when known) their date, the technique used, their dimensions, the place where they are currently housed, and the number of the page on which they appear. The numbers in bold type refer to the credits on page 64.

Abbreviations:
W = whole; D = detail.
o/c oil on canvas
RVGA Rijksmuseum Vincent van Gogh, Amsterdam
RKMO Rijksmuseum Kröller-Müller, Otterlo
MOP Musée d'Orsay, Paris

Anquetin, Louis
1 *Portrait of Emile Bernard,* c.1887, crayon on paper, 71 x 59 cm (28 x 23 in) (RVGA) 34 W
Bernard, Emile
2 *Breton Women in the Fields,* 1888, o/c, 74 x 92 cm (29 x 36 in) (Private collection) 35 D; **3** *Bridges at Asnières,* 1887, o/c, 45.9 x 54.2 cm (18 x 21 in) (Museum of Modern Art, New York) 26 W; **4** *Self-portrait, to my Friend Vincent,* 1888, o/c, 46.5 x 55.5 cm (18 x 22 in) (RVGA) 35 W
Boldini, Giovanni
5 *Portrait of Giuseppe Verdi,* 1886, crayon on paper, 65 x 54 cm (26 x 21 in) (Galleria Nazionale di Arte Moderna, Rome) 22 W
Braque, Georges
6 *Landscape at La Ciotat,* 1906 (Galerie Beyeler, Basel) 39 W
Breton, Jules
7 *The Return of the Gleaners,* 1859, o/c (MOP) 11 D
Cézanne, Paul
8 *Dr Gachet in the Studio,* 1873, charcoal on paper (Louvre, Paris) 55 W; **9** *Dr Gachet's House at Auvers,* 1873, o/c, 46 x 37.5 cm (18 x 15 in) (MOP) 55 W; **10** *Mont Sainte-Victoire,* c.1887, o/c (Courtauld Institute Galleries, London) 39 W
Courbet, Gustave
11 *Burial at Ornans,* 1849-50, o/c, 314 x 663 cm (124 x 261 in) (MOP) 10 W; **12** *Spring Mating Season,* 1861, o/c, 355 x 507 cm (140 x 200 in) (MOP) 11 W; **13** *The Vercingetorix Oak,* 1864, o/c, 89 x 129 cm (35 x 51 in) (Pennsylvania Academy of Fine Arts, Philadelphia) 11 W
Daumier, Honoré
14 *The Laundress,* 1860, oil on board, 49 x 33.5 cm (19 x 13 in) (MOP) 10 W
Degas, Edgar
15 *The Tub,* 1886, o/c, 60 x 83 cm (24 x 33 in) (MOP) 23 W
Derain, André
16 *Landscape at Collioure,* 1905, o/c, 81.3 x 100.3 cm (32 x 39 in) (National Gallery of Art, Washington) 60 W, D
Gachet, Paul
17 *Portrait of Vincent on his Deathbed,* 29 July 1890, crayon (MOP) 55 W
Gauguin, Paul
18 *Jacob's Struggle with the Angel,* 1888, o/c, 74.4 x 93.1 cm (29 x 37 in) (National Gallery of Scotland, Edinburgh) 49 W; **19** *Nevermore,* 1894, o/c (Courtauld Institute Galleries, London) 49 W; **20** *Oviri,* 1894, pottery, 75 x 19 x 27 cm (30 x 7 x 11 in) (MOP) 48 W; **21** *Portrait of Van Gogh Painting Sunflowers,* 1888, o/c, 73 x 91 cm (29 x 36 in) (RVGA) 40 W; **22** *Self-portrait (Les Misérables),* November 1888, o/c, 45 x 55 cm (18 x 22 in) (RVGA) 48 W; **23** *Self-portrait vase,* 1889, painted ceramic, height 19.3 cm (8 in) (Kunstindustrimuseet, Copenhagen); **24** *Vahine no te Tiare (Woman with Flower),* 1891, o/c, 70 x 46 cm (28 x 18 in) (Ny Carlsberg Glyptotek, Copenhagen) 48 W; **25** *Vase with Breton Scenes,* 1887-88, painted ceramic, height 29 cm (11 in) (Musée Royaux d'Art et d'Histoire, Brussels) 48 W
Gogh, Vincent van
26 *The Alpilles with Olive Trees in the Foreground,* June 1889, o/c, 72.5 x 92 cm (29 x 36 in) (Whitney Collection, New York) 51 W; **27** *L'Arlésienne,* Jan-Feb 1890, o/c, 65 x 54 cm (26 x 21 in) (Museu de Arte, São Paulo) 45 W; **28** *Bedroom in Arles,* 1888, o/c, 72 x 90 cm (28 x 35 in) (RVGA) 46-47 W, D; **29** *Bedroom in Arles,* sketch in a letter to Theo, Oct 1888, pen and ink on paper, 13.5 x 21 cm (5 x 8 in) (RVGA) 46 W; **30** *La Berceuse (Madame Roulin),* 1889 (Private collection) 44 W; **31** *Boulevard de Clichy,* 1887, o/c, 46.5 x 55 cm (18 x 22 in) (RVGA) 30-31 W, D; **32** *Boulevard de Clichy,* preparatory drawing, early 1887, pen, ink and coloured chalks on paper, 38 x 52.5 cm (15 x 21 in) (RVGA) 30 W; **33** *Bridges at Asnières,* 1887, o/c, 52 x 65 cm (20 x 26 in) (Bührle Collection, Zurich) 26-27 W, D; **34** *Café Terrace at Night,* 1888, o/c, 81 x 65.5 cm (32 x 26 in) (RKMO) 51 W, D; **35** *Chair with Pipe,* Dec 1888, o/c (National Gallery, London) 47 W; **36** *The Church at Auvers,* June 1890, o/c, 94 x 74 cm (37 x 29 in) (MOP) 58-59 W, D; **37** *Courtyard of the Arles Hospital,* April 1889, o/c, 73 x 92 cm (29 x 36 in) (Oscar Reinhart Collection, Winterthur) 52 W; **38** *Cypresses,* June 1889, o/c, 93.3 x 74 cm (37 x 29 in) (Metropolitan Museum of Art, New York) 51 W; **39** *Dr Gachet's Garden in Auvers,* May 1890, o/c, 54 x 101 cm (21 x 40 in) (MOP) 54 W; **40** *Fishing Boats on the Beach of Saintes-Maries,* 1888, o/c, 65 x 85.1 cm (26 x 34 in) (RVGA) 43 W; **41** *Fourteen Sunflowers in a Vase,* Jan 1889, o/c, 95 x 73 cm (37 x 29 in) (RVGA) 43 W; **42** *The Garden of Daubigny's House,* July 1890, o/c, 53 x 103 cm (21 x 41 in) (Öffentliche Kunstsammlung, Basel) 58 W; **43** *La Guinguette,* Oct 1886, o/c (MOP) 56 W; **44** *Gauguin's Chair,* Dec 1888, o/c, 90.5 x 72.5 cm (36 x 29 in) (RVGA) 47 W; **45** *Harvest on the Plain of La Crau,* 1888, o/c, 73 x 92 cm (29 x 36 in) (RVGA) 38 W; **46** *Haystacks in Provence,* 1888, o/c, 73 x 92.5 cm (29 x 36 in) (RKMO) 43 W; **47** *Head of a Peasant Woman,* May-June 1885, black chalk on onionskin, 40 x 33 cm (16 x 13 in) (RVGA) 15 W; **48** *House of the Coal Merchant,* Nov 1878, pencil, pen and ink on paper, 14 x 14.5 cm (5 x 6 in) (RVGA) 12 W; **49** *Interior of a Restaurant,* 1887, o/c, 45.5 x 56.5 cm (18 x 22 in) (RKMO) 31 W, D; **50** *Irises,* 1889, o/c (Paul Getty Museum, Malibu) 57 W; **51** *The Italian Woman,* Dec 1887, o/c, 81 x 60 cm (32 x 24 in) (MOP) 34 W; **52** *The Langlois Bridge with Women Washing,* March 1888, o/c, 54 x 65 cm (21 x 26 in) (RKMO) 38 D; **53** Letter to Theo on Goupil headed notepaper, 24 July 1875 (RVGA) 20; **54** *Moulin de Blute-fin,* summer 1886, o/c, 38.5 x 46 cm (15 x 18 in) (Art Gallery and Museum, Glasgow) 32 W; **55** *La Mousmé,* July 1888, o/c, 74 x 60 cm (29 x 24 in) (National Gallery of Art, Washington) 45 W; **56** *Peasant Woman with Spade,* Aug 1885 (Barber Institute of Fine Arts, Birmingham) 15 W; **57** *Peasants Seated around a Table,* 1890, pencil and black chalk on paper, 22.5 x 30.5 cm (9 x 12 in) (RVGA) 14 W; **58** *Pink Peach Tree in Blossom (Souvenir de Mauve),* 1888, o/c, 80.5 x 59.5 cm (32 x 23 in) (RKMO) 38 W; **59** *Portrait of Agostina Segatori at the Tambourin,* early 1887, o/c, 55.5 x 46.5 cm (22 x 18 in) (RVGA) 32 W; **60** *Portrait of the Art Dealer Alexander Reid,* 1887, o/c, 41 x 33 cm (16 x 13 in) (Art Gallery and Museum, Glasgow) 27 W; **61** *Portrait of Dr Félix Rey,* Jan 1889, o/c, 64 x 53 cm (25 x 21 in) (Pushkin Museum, Moscow) 52 W; **62** *Portrait of Dr Gachet,* June 1890, o/c, 67 x 56 cm (26 x 22 in) (Private collection) 54 W; **63** *Portrait of Dr Gachet,* June 1890, o/c, 68 x 57 cm (27 x 22 in) (MOP) 54-55 W, D; **64** *Portrait of Dr Gachet with Pipe,* May 1890, etching, 18 x 15 cm (7 x 6 in) (RKMO) 54 W; **65** *Portrait of Joseph Roulin,* July-Aug 1889, o/c, 81 x 65 cm (32 x 26 in) (Museum of Fine Arts, Boston) 44 W; **66** *Portrait of Père Tanguy,* autumn 1887, o/c, 65 x 51 cm (26 x 20 in) (Musée Rodin, Paris) 16 W; **67** *The Potato Eaters,* 1885, o/c, 81.5 x 114.5 cm (32 x 45 in) (RVGA) 14-15 W, D; **68** *The Potato Eaters,* 1885, lithograph, 26.5 x 30.5 cm (10 x 12 in) (RKMO) 14 W; **69** *The Public Garden in Place Lamartine with the Yellow House in the Background,* Sept 1888, pencil, quill, cane and ink on paper, 31.5 x 49.5 cm (12 x 19 in) (RVGA) 42 W; **70** *The Red Vineyard,* Nov 1888, o/c, 75 x 93 cm (30 x 37 in) (Pushkin Museum, Moscow) 56 W; **71** *Restaurant "La Sirène" at Asnières,* 1887, o/c, 54 x 65 cm (21 x 26 in) (MOP) 31 W; **72** *Return of the Miners,* 1880, 44.5 x 56 cm (18 x 22 in) (RKMO) 12 W; **73** *Riverbank at Asnières,* 1887, o/c, 49 x 65.5 cm (19 x 26 in) (RVGA) 27 W; **74** *Road with Steps in Auvers, with Figures,* May 1890, o/c, 49.8 x 70.1 cm (20 x 28 in) (Saint Louis Art Museum) 59 W; **75** *Self-portrait,* oil on paper, 34.2 x 25.5 cm (13 x 10 in) (RKMO) 36 W; **76** *Self-portrait,* 1889, o/c, 65 x 54 cm (26 x 21 in) (MOP) 37 W; **77** *Self-portrait in Front of the Easel,* 1888, o/c, 65.5 x 50.5 cm (26 x 20 in) (RVGA) 36-37 W, D; **78** *Self-portrait in Front of the Easel,* 1886, o/c, 46.5 x 38.5 cm (18 x 15 in) (RVGA) 36 W; **79** *Self-portrait with Bandaged Ear,* Jan 1889, o/c, 60 x 49 cm (24 x 19 in) (Courtauld Institute Galleries, London) 53 W; **80** *Self-portrait with Dark Hat,* 1886, o/c, 41.5 x 32.5 cm (41 x 13 in) (RVGA) 36 W; **81** *Self-portrait with Felt Hat,* 1887-88, o/c, 44 x 37.5 cm (17 x 15 in) (RVGA) 37 W; **82** *Self-portrait with Straw Hat and Pipe,* 1888, o/c on cardboard, 42 x 30 cm (17 x 12 in) (RVGA) 37 W; **83** *The Shoveller's Rest,* 1882 (Private collection) 13 W; **84** *Square in Ramsgate,* sketch in a letter to Theo, April 1876, pen and pencil on paper, 6.5 x 11 cm (2.5 x 4 in) (RVGA) 9 W; **85** *Starry Night,* 1889, o/c, 73.7 x 92.1 cm (29 x 36 in) (Museum of Modern Art, New York) 50-51 W, D; **86** *Starry Night,* 1889, drawing (Kunsthalle, Bremen) 50 W; **87** *Starry Night on the Rhône,* 1888, o/c, 72.5 x 92 cm (29 x 36 in) (MOP) 49 W, 51 D; **88** *Still Life with Bible,* 1885, o/c, 65 x 78 cm (26 x 31 in) (RVGA) 19 W; **89** *Still Life with Bottles,* 1884-85, o/c, 33 x 41 cm (13 x 16 in) (RKMO) 41 W; **90** *Still Life with Clock and Clog,* 1885, black chalk on paper, 27 x 18.5 cm (11 x 7 in) (RVGA) 18 W; **91** *Still Life with Clogs,* 1885, oil on board, 39 x 41.5 cm (15 x 16 in) (RKMO) 19 W, D; **92** *Still Life with Drawing Board,* Jan 1889, o/c, 50 x 64 cm (20 x 25 in) (RKMO) 41 W; **93** *Still Life with Plate of Lemons and Carafe,* 1887, o/c, 46.5 x 38.5 cm (18 x 14 in) (RVGA) 27 W, 41 D; **94** *Still Life with Straw Hat,* 1885, o/c, 36 x 53.5 cm (14 x 21 in) (RKMO) 18-19 W, D; **95** *The Town Hall at Auvers on 14 July,* 1890, o/c, 72 x 93 cm (28 x 37 in) (Private collection) 58 D; **96** *Two Self-portraits: Fragments of a Third,* 1887, pen, pencil and ink on onionskin, 31.6 x 24.1 cm (12 x 9 in) (RVGA) 36 W; **97** *Vegetable Gardens in Montmartre,* 1887, o/c, 96 x 120 cm (38 x 47 in) (Stedelijk Museum, Amsterdam) 30 W; **98** *View of the Port of Antwerp,* 1885, o/c, 20.5 x 27 cm (8 x 11 in) (RVGA) 17 W; **99** *Wheatfield with Crows,* Jul 1890, o/c, 50.3 x 103 cm (20 x 41 in) (RVGA) 59 W, 60 D; **100** *Worshippers Leaving the Church at Nuenen,* Jan 1884, o/c, 41.5 x 32 cm (16 x 13 in) (RVGA) 6 W; **101** *The Yellow House,* 1888, o/c, 72 x 91.5 cm (28 x 36 in) (RVGA) 42-43 W, D; **102** *The Yellow House,* Sept-Oct 1888, watercolour, 25.5 x 31.5 cm (10 x 12 in) (RVGA) 42 W
Guigou, Paul
103 *The Hills of Allauch near Marseille,* 1863 (Musée des Beaux-Arts, Marseille) 39 W
Hals, Frans
104 *Banquet of the Officers of the Militia Company of St George,* 1616 (Frans Halsmuseum, Haarlem) 19 D
Heckel, Erich
105 *Brickwork,* 1907, o/c, 68 x 86 cm (27 x 34 in) (Thyssen Foundation, Madrid) 61 W, D
Hiroshige, Ando
106 *The Bridge of Kyoto in the Light of the Moon,* print from *One Hundred Views of Edo,* 1856-59, 17 W
Israëls, Jozef
107 *Inside a Hovel,* 1890, o/c, 104 x 134 cm (41 x 53 in) (MOP) 15 D
Kirchner, Ernst Ludwig
108 *Woman in a Birch Wood,* 1906 (Thyssen Foundation, Madrid) 60 W
Luce, Maximilien
109 *Paris from Montmartre,* 1887, o/c, 65 x 54 cm (26 x 21 in) (Musée du Petit Palais, Geneva) 29 W, D
Manet, Edouard
110 *Portrait of Emile Zola,* 1868, o/c, 146 x 114 cm (57 x 45 in) (MOP) 10 D, 16 W
Matisse, Henri
111 *Landscape at Collioure,* 1905, o/c (Musée de l'Annonciade, Saint-Tropez) 39 W; **112** *View of Collioure,* 1905, 59 x 73 cm (23 x 29 in) (Hermitage, St Petersburg) 60 W
Maufra, Maxime
113 *Landscape at Pont-Aven,* 1890 (Musée des Beaux-Arts, Quimper) 49 W
Mauve, Anton
114 *The Seaweed Gatherer,* o/c, 51 x 71 cm (20 x 28 in) (MOP) 7 W
Millet, Jean-François
115 *The Gleaners,* 1857, o/c, 85.5 x 111 cm (34 x 44 in) (MOP) 11 W; **116** *Spring,* 1868-73, o/c, 131 x 88 cm (52 x 35 in) (MOP) 11 W
Monet, Claude
117 *Woman with Parasol,* 1886, o/c, 131 x 88 cm (52 x 35 in) (MOP) 22 D
Munch, Edvard
118 *Starry Night,* 1924-25, o/c, 120.5 x 100 cm (47 x 39 in) (Munch Museet, Oslo) 61 W
Nolde, Emil
119 *In the Wheat,* 1906, o/c, 65 x 82 cm (26 x 32 in) (Nolde Foundation, Seebüll) 61 W
Pissarro, Camille
120 *The Gleaners,* 1889, o/c, 65.5 x 81 cm (26 x 32 in) (Öffentliche Kunstsammlung, Basel) 22 D
Renoir, Pierre-Auguste
121 *The Great Bathers,* 1884-87, o/c, 118 x 170.5 cm (46 x 67 in) (Museum of Art, Philadelphia) 23 W
Rousseau, Henri (known as Le Douanier)
122 *Carnival Night,* 1886, o/c, 116 x 89 cm (46 x 35 in) (Museum of Art, Philadelphia) 23 D; **123** *A Riverbank,* 1886, o/c, 21 x 39 cm (8 x 15 in) (Private collection, Paris) 23 W; **124** *Self-portrait – Landscape,* 1889-90, o/c, 143 x 110.5 cm (56 x 44 in) (Národni Galerie, Prague) 25 D
Rousseau, Théodore
125 *Morning in the Forest of Fontainebleau,* 1850 (Wallace Collection, London) 11 W
Rubens, Peter Paul
126 *Self-portrait with his Wife, Isabella Brant,* 1609-10 (Alte Pinakothek, Munich) 17 W
Russell, John Peter
127 *Portrait of Van Gogh,* 1886, o/c, 60 x 45 cm (24 x 18 in) (RVGA) 37 W
Sérusier, Paul
128 *The Talisman,* 1888, o/c, 27 x 21 cm (11 x 8 in) (MOP) 49 D
Seurat, Georges
129 *The Circus,* 1890-91, o/c, 185.5 x 152.5 cm (73 x 60 in) (MOP) 33 W; **130** *The Circus Parade,* 1887-88, o/c, 99.7 x 150 cm (39 x 59 in) (Metropolitan Museum of Art, New York) 28 W, D; **131** *La Grande Jatte,* 1884-86, o/c, 207 x 308 cm (81 x 121 in) (Art Institute, Chicago) 23 W
Signac, Paul
132 *The Dining Room,* 1886-87, o/c, 89 x 115 cm (35 x 45 in) (RKMO) 23 D; **133** *The Lighthouse at Portrieux,* 1888 (Private collection) 29 W, D; **134** *Saint-Tropez – Storm,* 1895, o/c, 46 x 55 cm (18 x 21 in) (Musée de l'Annonciade, Saint-Tropez) 39 W
Toulouse-Lautrec, Henri de
135 *Carmen,* 1884, 52.8 x 40.8 cm (21 x 16 in) (Sterling and Francine Clark Art Institute, Williamstown, Massachusetts) 34 W; **136** *Moulin Rouge, La Goulue,* 1891, lithograph, 193 x 122 cm (76 x 48 in) (Victoria and Albert Museum, London) 33 W; **137** *Portrait of the Countess de Toulouse-Lautrec,* 1886-87 (Musée Lautrec, Albi) 34 W
Troyon, Constant
138 *The Pointer,* 1860 (Museum of Fine Arts, Boston) 10 W
Viesseux
139 *Portrait of Gustave Eiffel* (MOP) 24 W
Vlaminck, Maurice
140 *Houses and Trees,* 1906, o/c, 54.3 x 65.4 cm (21 x 26 in) (Metropolitan Museum of Art, New York) 61 W, D
Ward, Edward Matthew
141 *Portrait of Queen Victoria* (Forbes Magazine Collection, New York) 8 W

♦ INDEX

♦ CREDITS

The original and previously unpublished illustrations in this book may be reproduced only with the prior permission of Donati Giudici Associati, who hold the copyright.

ILLUSTRATIONS

Simone Boni, pp. 12-13, 24-25; Francesca D'Ottavi, pp. 4-5, 6-7, 8-9, 32-33, 34-35, 44-45; L. R. Galante, pp. 20-21, 52-53; Ivan Stalio, pp. 16-17, 40-41, 56-57.
COVER: L.R. Galante.
BACK COVER AND TITLE PAGE: Francesca D'Ottavi.

WORKS OF ART REPRODUCED

Alinari/Giraudon: 6, 27, 95, 103, 112, 123, 124, 137; Art Institute, Chicago: 131; Bridgeman Art Library: 2, 10, 13, 18, 19, 30, 34, 35, 37, 38, 50, 54, 55, 56, 60, 61, 62, 65, 70, 79, 83, 106, 108, 113, 120, 125, 136, 141; Bührle Collection, Zurich: 33; DoGi: 11, 115; Eric Lessing, Vienna: 24, 39, 66, 104, 118, 126, 129, 133; Galleria Nazionale d'Arte Moderna, Rome: 5; Kunsthalle, Bremen: 86; Kunstindustrimuseet, Copenhagen: 23; Metropolitan Museum of Art, New York: 130, 140; Musée du Petit Palais, Geneva: 109; Musée Royaux d'Art et d'Histoire, Brussels: 25; Museum of Art, Philadelphia: 121, 122; Museum of Fine Arts, Boston: 138; Museum of Modern Art, New York: 3, 85; National Gallery of Art, Washington: 16; Nolde Foundation, Seebüll: 119; Öffentliche Kunstsammlung, Basel: 42; Rijksmuseum Kröller-Müller, Otterlo: 46, 49, 52, 58, 64, 72, 75, 89, 91, 92, 94, 132; Rijksmuseum Vincent van Gogh (Van Gogh Foundation), Amsterdam: 1, 4, 21, 22, 28, 29, 31, 32, 40, 41, 44, 45, 47, 48, 53, 57, 59, 67, 68, 69, 73, 77, 78, 80, 81, 82, 84, 88, 90, 93, 96, 98, 99, 100, 101, 102, 127; RMN: 7, 8, 9, 12, 14, 15, 17, 20, 36, 43, 51, 63, 71, 76, 87, 107, 110, 111, 114, 116, 117, 128, 134, 139; Saint-Louis Art Museum, Saint-Louis: 74; Stedelijk Museum, Amsterdam: 97; Sterling and Francine Clark Art Institute, Williamstown, Massachusetts:135; Thyssen Foundation, Madrid: 105; Whitney Collection, New York: 26.
COVER (clockwise): Alinari/Giraudon: j, n; Bridgeman Art Library: d, q, r, u;

Rijksmuseum Vincent van Gogh (Van Gogh Foundation), Amsterdam: a, b, e, g, i, k, l, p, s, v, w, x; Rijksmuseum Vincent van Gogh, Otterlo: o, RMN: c, f, h, m.

DOCUMENTS

Bridgeman Art Library: pp. 9, 25; © Collection Viollet: pp. 32, 56; Einaudi Archive: pp. 28c, 29tr; Harlingue-Viollet: pp. 33, 53, 54; Insel Archive: p. 53; ND-Viollet: p. 24; Rijksmuseum Vincent van Gogh (Van Gogh Foundation), Amsterdam: pp. 7cl, 7cr, 20t, 22c, 26b, 40b, 44t; Roger Viollet: p. 58.
BACK COVER: Rijksmuseum Vincent van Gogh (Van Gogh Foundation), Amsterdam.

Works by Heckel, Kirchner, Matisse, Munch, Nolde and Vlaminck have been reproduced with the authorization of the Società Italiana degli Autori ed Editori, 1996. © Succession Matisse by SIAE, 1996. © The Munch-Museum/The Munch-Ellingsen Group by SIAE, 1996.